FIRE

A Life of Faith Adventure

William L. Sage

Trilogy Christian Publishers

A Wholly Owned Subsidiary of Trinity Broadcasting Network

2442 Michelle Drive

Tustin, CA 92780

10 9 8 7 6 5 4 3 2 1

Library of Congress Cataloging-in-Publication Data is available.

ISBN 979-8-89333-787-7

ISBN (ebook) 979-8-89333-788-4

Endorsements for *Wings of Fire*

This amazing true tale about Bill and Shirley's adventure into business is entertaining and educational! I am an eyewitness to the results in their lives and business. Almost everyone in America has seen the impact of their business with their own eyes. Whether you are a person who appreciates the American entrepreneur's spirit, or the efforts involved in starting and growing a business, or perhaps are even a young or aspiring writer, read this book!

Ron Wood, Author

Bill Sage was a Christian businessman that understood we are all ministers in Christ's kingdom. He was a humble man that possessed extraordinary faith. As the Holy Spirit led him, he prayed for many sick people who were miraculously healed and restored. This book and its testimonies will grow your faith and challenge you to step out to be used by the Holy Spirit, extending the ministry of Jesus to a world desperately in need of Him.

Dr. Tony Nichols, Senior Pastor of Church Alive, Northwest Arkansas

William Lee Sage was born in 1944 and lived in several states, including Minnesota, Illinois, California, and Arkansas. In 1979, an unexpected open vision changed everything he thought he knew about God. His faith adventure will challenge you to examine how God works in our lives.

Foreword

So many times, people have told me that I should write a book. I love sharing with friends, relatives, and people I have never met before what the Lord has done in my life. For nearly three years or more I have pondered their suggestion. The only answer I seem to come up with is a question: should a man live his life in the blessing of the Lord and not tell it? Or, should a man live his life and die and not pass on the great hope that is within?

I believe that the stories I share of how God has miraculously intervened in my life are mere reflections of the untold stories in the lives of many others.

I write this book not only to have a written record that I can pass down to my children and grandchildren, but also to encourage the body of Christ.

Certainly, God is no respecter of persons and what He has done for me, He will do for you.

The following stories and events are written as the Holy Spirit brings them to mind. If you are a believer of the Word of God, then what I tell you will ring true. If you have strong religious traditions, you may struggle with it, but I would entreat you to keep an open mind. And, if you are seeking to learn more about God, are perhaps even offended by what you see in us who call ourselves Christians, then I would ask that you also read with an open mind.

It is my hope that you will be blessed by what you read and will want more of God.

You may say, "Who is this guy?" Truly you know me, not by my face but by what I have brought to this world. I will share with you how God moved in my life to bring this product to you. I will also share how God has used me to be a blessing to others. I write this so that your faith in Jesus Christ, the one and only living Son of God, will be watered and enhanced. And I write this so that those who have not responded to God's calling will search their hearts and seek God while He is still calling.

PREFACE

The Bible is a compilation of stories of how God revealed Himself to men, women, and nations over several thousand years. God moved mightily through prophets of old and through New Testament Christians. In His appointed time, God sent His Word, Jesus Christ, to save men from the god of this world, the devil himself.

Jesus said, "I came that you might have life, and have that life more abundantly." He also said, "I came to destroy the works of the devil."

In addition, He let us know that it was the devil, not God, whose primary function in this world is to steal, kill, and destroy.

As a young child and later as an adult, the devil tried to kill me at least twelve times. Once by chemical burns, once by fire, once by automobile accident, once by a boat accident, five times by airplane incidents, twice by electrocution, and once by mercury poisoning. When I think about it, it is a miracle I am alive today. And I was not preaching, nor did I have any revelation of the Word like the Apostle Paul to make the devil mad. I was too young and not born again when these events took place. I did not know it was the devil who hated me and wanted me out of the way.

As you read this book you will see how he nearly destroyed our finances and how he tried to steal my health. But I am thankful for the calling of the Holy Spirit who led me to the one and only Savior, Jesus Christ. If it wasn't for a faithful wife praying for me, I'm not sure I would have ever answered God's call.

When I was only four years old, my brother and I had a bedroom in the basement of our house in St. Louis Park, Minnesota. The bedroom had a large picture window that overlooked a small wood. One day in early spring several big black flies had gathered around that picture window. Bob and I woke up to the buzzing sound of the flies.

We talked about how bothersome they were and devised a foolproof plan on how to get rid of them. Next to our bedroom was Dad's workshop. In it he had lots of stuff in cans and bottles. We found an old two-pound coffee can and began pouring gasoline, turpentine, paint thinner and other liquids into the can. Certain that this mixture would kill the flies, we took the can to the window sill and began catching flies and throwing them in.

The flies were somewhat overcome by the fumes. We watched them dance around on the top of the surface of our concoction. After a while, we realized that the flies were not dying. So one of us had the bright idea of lighting it.

When we brought the match close to the can, both of us got a huge surprise!

There was a loud "PHOOM!" sound as the fire sucked up the surrounding air and flames shot up all the way to the ceiling! No doubt the flies were dead, but I would have given anything to have seen the look on our faces. My first thought was: "What have we done now?" I looked at Bob, and he looked at me, as we tried to decide what to do. It was about six o'clock Sunday morning and we didn't want to wake Mom and Dad.

I yelled, "Let's dump it down the utility sink!" Bob agreed by grabbing the coffee can around the middle. I turned in front of him and ran towards the sink. I was going to turn the water on to put out the flames. Unfortunately for me, I was too close to Bob and he tripped, causing the can of flames from hell to pour onto me. I was wearing a tee shirt and pajamas. They went

up in flames. I began screaming as the flames burned my hair, arms, neck and back. I was able to get out of the burning pajamas, but by the time I grabbed my tee shirt the only thing left was the collar.

Needless to say, by then I had done a good job of waking up my parents. I was yelling so loud the whole neighborhood could have heard me. Mom called the doctor as

I waited on the side of her bed. I couldn't lie down due to the pain. Blisters were forming on my arms, hand, and back. When the doctor came, he was very gentle and had a cream that soothed the pain. The miracle is that I lived, and the better part is that I did not end up with any visible long-lasting scars.

Not long after that experience, I was once again playing in Dad's workshop. He had an old floor lamp next to his workbench. Curious to see it turn on, I plugged it in. I was holding the metal pole while holding onto the electric cord. The moment I plugged it in, my body became the pathway for the current. I was being electrocuted. I couldn't let go, and I couldn't say a word.

My hand was frozen to the pole and the electric cord. By the grace of God, my mother happened to enter the room seconds after I plugged the cord in.

Mom yelled out something like: "Billy, are you okay?" I couldn't answer, so she immediately unplugged the cord. Again, my life was spared.

When I was in my mid-thirties, prior to a wakeup call by God, Shirley and I were flying in a twin engine airplane from California to Minnesota. I was the pilot in command, or so I thought. We left the Van Nuys airport the day after the airplane had a fresh annual checkup. Licensed airplane mechanics had just finished a thorough inspection of the airplane. So I was confident in the integrity of the old Twin Beech.

As we approached Las Vegas, we had to land due to a hurricane-like storm that was further ahead of our flight path through Salt Lake City, Utah. We spent the night in Las Vegas and left the next morning, thinking the storm was well out of our way. As I flew over Salt Lake City the weather was fine, but I could see clouds ahead. The weather report said that Cheyenne, Wyoming was good for visual flight rules and that was our intended destination that day.

As I went through the mountain passes, it was necessary for me to climb. As

I began to climb, I found myself skirting the clouds. I knew it was necessary to stay clear of the clouds so I decided since the weather was good, I would climb above the clouds. This was a big mistake. The clouds started to close in, leaving no visibility of the ground. I was not rated to fly using instruments only at that time. I could not fly in instrument conditions.

I asked Shirley to hand me the oxygen mask as I was approaching 11,500 feet. Suddenly the left engine started missing. I thought, "Oh God, what is happening?" I didn't say anything to Shirley, because I did not want to frighten her, since she was holding our one-year-old son. The engine kept running, but I was prepared to feather it if that became necessary. And then all of a sudden, I noticed that the fuel gauge was dropping abnormally fast.

Fortunately, a large hole in the clouds appeared. I lowered the flaps and landing gear and began a slow, controlled spiral down out of the clouds. Soon I could see a highway below me and followed it all the way to Cheyenne. Upon landing, I taxied up to the fixed base operator where I summoned a mechanic. Together we walked around the plane and saw a huge green stain under the right wing.

Upon further examination, we found that the right fuel bowl had come loose.

High octane fuel was pouring out the right side of the engine as we were flying. This, of course, was the reason for the unusual rapid drop I saw on the fuel gauge.

We left the airplane overnight for the mechanics to check out. In the morning, we found out that the left engine had swallowed a valve due to an over-lean mixture of fuel. The company that had done our annual inspection did not do a proper job of equalizing the fuel during the inspection, nor did they properly seat the fuel bowl on the right engine.

From that information, it was highly likely I could have lost both engines or worse yet, the airplane could have caught on fire and blown up in midair.

I called my dad, who was in California, and told him about the recent incident. He told me a grisly story about another pilot who that same day was flying a Beechcraft QueenAir that had caught on fire in the wheel well and blown up!

Through all these experiences, could it be that God had intervened to spare my life so that I might bring something important to this world? If it had been God, I was not looking in His direction. As a matter of fact, I didn't think twice about all the events that could have put me in the ground short of a full life span.

It was around the time of this incident that I began wondering about my life and my reason for existence. I didn't know God had a plan for my life until He grabbed my attention with a vision.

Chapter 1
THE VISION

In my early twenties, I taught in elementary and junior high schools. As a ninth-grade science teacher, I was particularly interested in teaching and learning about the universe. I wondered how it all got here and why. There was a time in my mid-thirties when I wondered about life, and my life in particular. I never came to any solid conclusions until God intervened.

One day while driving home in a new sports car, I stopped at the top of the driveway and with great satisfaction sat there to appreciate the scene before me. My wife and I had purchased a home situated on the eighteenth green of the Woodland Hills golf course in Woodland Hills, California.

Spread out before me was this wonderful home, a new car, and a beautiful fairway and a green. But the thought came to me, "Is that all there is?" I wondered what else there was in life. How about another new car, bigger and more powerful, or how about a new home, bigger and better? Suddenly the joy of the moment brought me back to the basic question running through my mind: "What is the meaning of life, and why am I here"?

At the time I didn't know what I was dealing with, but later on I came to find out it was the Holy Spirit drawing me to Jesus. I was seeking something to fill the emptiness in my life. I thought it was the accumulation of new, bigger, and better things that brought joy. But there for a moment, I paused as I contemplated the reason. And I put this incident into my memory because it was one of those moments that was…different.

My wife, Shirley, was a devout Christian. Ever since we were married, she had been attending the Bel Air Presbyterian Church. While there, she had joined a prayer team. What I didn't know was that every Thursday morning they would meet, and for nine years they were praying for me. In fact, they were praying that God would open my eyes to spiritual things, and, that as a result, that I would come to know Him. In light of that moment and my unending curiosity of my reason for existence, I would have to say that her prayers were working.

When we met, I had told her I was a Christian. I wasn't lying, but I wasn't living a Christian life. As far as the world was concerned, I was not a Christian. The fact was, I didn't understand the Bible. As a science teacher I didn't believe in things I couldn't see. But I was moved to ask Jesus to come into my heart while attending a Young Life camp in Colorado as a teen. That was the beginning and end of any religious experience I had known until I met Shirley.

Sunday morning would come each week, and she would gather the children together and go to church. I, on the other hand, would spend the time at the airport. My dad and I had purchased several airplanes over those nine years Shirley was praying for me. I enjoyed not only learning about flying, but also spending time flying to nearby airports to practice takeoffs and landings or to stop and have breakfast or lunch.

When Shirley came home, I would ask her how church went. It was my curiosity rising up about spiritual things, but I never got the answers I was seeking from her. Many times, I would question her about what the Bible said only to culminate in an argument. Usually, I would ask her if she believed in angels. She would say that she did but couldn't prove they existed. As an ex-science teacher, I had to have proof that I could see, hear, smell, taste or touch. I couldn't see angels. I lived in the realm of the senses.

And then sometimes I would say what my dad told me, "Christianity is only for those who need a crutch." Or I would argue that the only reason the church exists is to get your money. I'll bet you have heard all these arguments before.

Needless to say, Shirley was disappointed in my spiritual advancement. To her, it must have seemed like God was not hearing her prayers. But God was listening, and God had a big surprise in store for me. What God did changed my life, so much so, I will never look back at that old life.

It happened on June 18th, 1979. My dad and I had been planning to move our small business from California to somewhere in the Midwest. We wanted to find a simpler life away from the hustle and bustle of the big city.

My children were three and a half and one and a half years old. For the past five years, Dad and I had been looking in Arkansas and the surrounding area.

Usually after attending trade shows for our product in Dallas, we would fly up to Fort Smith, Arkansas. We would rent a car and search for a place to move our business. For four years we had done this, and we had not had any success in finding the right location. But on June 18th of 1979, Shirley and I made the trip from California to Arkansas. We had rented a home in

Bella Vista, Arkansas which was situated in the heart of the Ozark Mountains in the northwest corner of the state.

We had been dropping our two children off at a babysitter's home while we explored the Ozarks. I had put together a long list of things that I felt were necessary in order to make the move of our business successful. Dad was a recluse and somewhat of a survivalist. He wanted to find property that had its own stream, so that we could generate our own electricity if we needed it. He was tired of the fires, floods, mudslides and earthquakes we had been experiencing in California. We also wanted property located on a paved highway not too far from a town.

As Shirley and I searched for our dream property, it became clear to me that what I was looking for didn't exist. Everything we found was either too expensive or too far from town. We had spent an entire week covering every road in Northwest Arkansas and came up with nothing. I was very frustrated and tired. I felt like our dream was not to be. But then, I had a thought...

"Maybe I should pray about it?"

We had just returned to our rented house, and Shirley was combing her hair in preparation for picking up the kids. I went to her and told her how disappointed I was. She looked at me and said: "Why don't you pray about it?"

Usually, I would argue and ask what good that would do, but this time I felt different about her comment, which I knew was motivated by her strong Christian belief. I thought to myself, "All right, I will. I will go and find out if there is a God. And, if there is one, does He really care? Does He even hear our prayers?"

I was determined in my heart to find out once and for all whether or not God truly existed. Well, as I have said, what happened floored me. He answered.

But not in a way I would have expected. But He did answer in a way that I later found out was exactly according to what He had spoken through the prophet Joel and later reiterated by the Apostle Peter in the book of Acts.

I wandered off to the bedroom and lay down on the bed. I looked up towards the ceiling and began what I felt in my heart was a humble prayer. I asked God to forgive me for my ungodly life and for not coming to Him sooner. But before I could go any further in my prayer, God intervened.

Normally a person would probably close his eyes when he prayed. I, on the other hand, was staring at the ceiling. My eyes were wide open when suddenly the ceiling began to open up. It started at the middle and expanded outwards toward the walls. I would guess that the hole was about six feet in diameter. The white ceiling instantly became blue sky, with a tree in its full array of green spring colors hanging over the hole.

Before I could even think about what was happening,

I felt a light sensation in my body. And suddenly I was no longer in my body but was transported to a distant location. I was fully aware that my body was still lying on the bed, but part of me was now miles away. I was brought to a location near Beaver Lake, perhaps twenty miles from where we were staying in Bella Vista.

I found myself looking over a vast expanse of the Ozark Mountains. All the trees, maples and oaks, were decked out in splendid fall colors. I was amazed at the bright reds and yellows. I realized that I was standing in mid-air about twenty feet above the trees.

As I looked across the mountains, I noticed three buildings about one hundred yards in front of me. The closest of the three was a small white building that appeared to be a storage shed. The next building was to the right and it was larger and was painted brown. The building in the center appeared to be a home and it was painted white. Beyond these buildings was a valley. I could see the tree line drop in the distance and then rise up again on the distant ridge. What I didn't know until later was that between the buildings and the distant ridge was a beautiful lake called Beaver Lake.

Suddenly I found myself back in the bedroom. I was once again aware of my body lying on the bed. My body felt kind of a sinking feeling as I entered it again. I noticed the ceiling close up in much the same manner as an old television picture tube used to shut off. There was a gray circle that closed up into a small black dot and then disappeared.

I immediately became aware of my entire being present on the bed in that room, and I felt the presence of another person whom I could not see. I felt a weight upon my chest like someone laying his hand upon me. And then the entire experience was over.

Needless to say, I had never in my life experienced anything like what just happened! I was silent upon that bed for quite some time as I contemplated the entire experience. I knew I was there to seek God, but the thought that

God had just intervened in my life really didn't catch hold. I was more interested in the experience than the realization that God was working in me.

I was so taken aback and puzzled I didn't know what to make of it.

I thought this was crazy, but then I thought it was necessary to tell Shirley what had happened. My thinking was that if I didn't tell her, and we should happen to come across the property I just saw, she wouldn't believe I had this experience. I therefore rose up out of bed and went to find Shirley, who was still combing her hair.

I told her everything that happened. I described in detail all that I had seen. Then, thinking that something spiritual had happened to me,

I asked her what she thought it meant. Her reply was not what I expected. I was expecting a long dissertation on the Bible and how God speaks to people but instead she simply said, "I don't know."

We left our rented home to pick up our children. All that evening I pondered over the experience I had had. I didn't know then that the Bible tells us that we are triune beings. I knew that I had a body and a soul, but I thought the soul was that part that left the body when you died. And being around Christians as I grew up, I thought your soul either went to heaven or hell.

This, I found out later, is true too, but there is another part that makes man a special created being and that part is the spirit of man. I learned later that the spirit is the "inner man" or the real you. I also learned that the soul is made up of the mind, will, and emotions of man. I didn't know that it was my spirit that left my body.

I also didn't know that the Apostle Peter, in the book of Acts, spoke about what the prophet Joel had prophesied. He also told the people of Israel that in the latter days God would pour out his Spirit upon all mankind, and that their young men would see visions and their old men dream dreams. I didn't know that the experience I had was a "vision" until I read it later in the Bible.

The next morning, Shirley and I dropped our children off at the babysitter's.

This was the last day of vacation I had before we were to begin our return trip to California. There was a realtor in Garfield who had a neat looking office that was situated in a small round building. I thought I would like to stop in there and see if he might have the special piece of property I had been searching for.

When we arrived, the realtor was not in, but his secretary was sitting at her desk. I described to her the type of property I wanted. I did not tell her about the vision I had the night before, nor did I describe that property. My mind was still set on finding the right piece of land to which we could move our business from California.

She said they did not have anything listed that fit my description. But she did say that they had a beautiful home on Beaver Lake. I told her I wasn't interested in that home because I needed a place for our business. Shirley immediately became in tune with the conversation, and I believe in light of the vision I had, she felt there might be a connection.

The secretary said she had a stack of pictures on the realtor's desk and asked if we would like to see them. I was still not aware of any spiritual connection and told the lady again that I wasn't interested in seeing the pictures. But Shirley stopped me and encouraged me to at least take a look.

It was springtime in the Ozarks as we stood in the lobby of that small round building. Outside was a sign that read "Lakewood Realty." It was nestled against the bank next to the highway that ran past. Across the highway and just about everywhere you looked you could see how lush and green the Ozarks are in the spring.

The lady handed me the stack of pictures. What I saw on the first picture was a view of the Ozarks in the fall, with beautiful fall colors in the trees.

Suddenly this caught my attention, because in the vision were beautiful maples and oaks in fall colors. As Shirley and I looked through the pictures, we were amazed when we reached the fourth picture. It was a picture of a small white building. "That's it, isn't it?" she blurted out.

I said, "Yes, that is it." Now that stack of pictures suddenly had our fullest attention.

As we proceeded through the stack of pictures, everything I had described to Shirley began to unfold right before our eyes. Needless to say, I was once again dumbfounded. The buildings, the trees, the valley, and the ridge all came into view in those pictures. I couldn't explain it in a three-dimension world.

What just happened had to involve another dimension that I was totally in the dark about.

About this time the realtor walked in. We introduced ourselves and told him that we were there to find property for our business and family. I explained that my father and mother also lived in California, and we had been planning a move to this region of the country.

He asked us if we would be interested in seeing the home and property shown in the pictures. In the excitement of what was happening, I answered him by telling him that I had already seen the property. He assured me that I had not, because he was the exclusive listing agent, and that no one could have seen or could see the property without his or the owner's permission.

I said, "I just saw it last night in a… vision!" And then I began to explain what had happened. He immediately took about three steps backwards. I could tell that this had also caught him off guard. So I told him I was not a religious man, but that I could not help what had happened. He seemed to be a little unnerved, but made plans to take us to the property.

Shirley and I had brought with us a video camera. Back in 1979, video cameras were very expensive and very large. They looked much like what you see your local television news cameramen carry today. When we arrived at the property, we had to travel down a paved driveway. It was about seven tenths of a mile long. We videoed the ride as the realtor drove. The driveway wound its way through tall oak trees on this warm spring day.

Shortly we came upon the small white storage building and then the brown building, which turned out to be a remote garage. The house sat in the middle, and was a long, low and modern home built out over the hillside. Beyond the house was Beaver Lake. Everything came together just like I had seen it in the vision.

We had never seen such a beautiful place. As a child, I had the wonderful experience of growing up in Minnesota and living on a lake.

Thoughts of those wonderful moments rose up within me, but the thought of ever being able to own this home quickly dashed my hopes. I asked the realtor how much they wanted and it was way beyond my means. I told him I would have to think about it and that I would get back to him the next day.

Now I was really confused. I had come to Arkansas to find a place from which to establish our business. I didn't want expensive lake property, especially something that looked like it was made for a king. But I was faced with the reality of the vision I had and seeing it actually unfold in front of me.

As we headed back to our rented home, I again pondered what was taking place. Once we reached home, I asked Shirley once again what it all meant. She said to me, "Bill, God is trying to tell you something." Well, if you are a Christian you probably already figured this out. I was spiritually cold, but the instant she said this I understood.

I said to her, "Do you mean God cares about me? She said yes, He did. And then again, I said, "Do you mean that out of billions of people on this planet God cares about *me*?" She said yes. I was caught hands down, flat footed.

The proverbial light bulb went off in my head. God was alive. God existed. God cares! After all, didn't I go to God in prayer? Didn't I seek Him for an answer to my problem? Didn't He answer me in His way?

At that moment I felt the love of God all over me. I felt so shameful. I realized God knew everything about me. He knew the good in me, and He knew the bad in me. He knew me well enough that He would answer me with a vision of what He knew I needed, and what would be useful for Him as I grew in my relationship with Him.

Shirley, sensing that her prayers were being answered, reached into her purse and pulled out a small book. She had been carrying it around with her ever since she left San Jose State College, where she was involved with Campus Crusade. I began weeping as the love of God surrounded me. She handed me the book of John and encouraged me to read it.

There in that small, rented home, I began reading what the Apostle John had written. As I read, I wept. For the first time in my life, I was able to read the Bible and understand. I understood the reason for God sending His only Son to die on the cross for me. I understood the dimension God lived in and why eternal life is so real. All the while as I read that evening, and for nearly four months after, as I read the Bible, I wept. I was being washed by the Word. My soul was being cleansed and my spirit was being fed the Word of God.

The next morning, I knew I had told the realtor that I would call him back and I did. There was no denying that God had intervened in my life, and in my mind I believed that if it was truly God calling, then I had better respond.

I told the realtor that we were prepared to make an offer on the home.

Personally, I thought I was absolutely nuts to even consider making an offer, but I believed in my heart that if this was God, He would supply whatever I needed.

I called my dad and explained to him in detail what had happened to me. He was naturally shocked. He was almost speechless. I am sure he must have thought I was caught up in some kind of religious cult or something. I told him even if I purchased the home, I would continue to look for the property he wanted and needed for our business.

Shirley and I met with the realtor and made an offer. Shirley, having also witnessed the experience I encountered, was in full support. But we were both wondering how in the world we would ever be able to afford such a magnificent home. We made the offer contingent upon the sale of our home in California, and I believe we had six months in which to complete the sale.

The elderly person who owned the property was willing to finance the balance of the sale, which made it easier for us.

After returning to California, we began to pray in earnest every night that God would bring us a buyer. We watched the video we had taken and reviewed the photos of the property many times. It consisted of over sixty-six acres of prime real estate on Beaver Lake. The house was approximately thirty-six hundred square feet overlooking the lake, with nearly three quarters of a mile of lake shore. Everything about it was a dream that we hoped would come true.

In contrast, we were living in an older one-level home. It had about twenty-four hundred square feet of living space and a car port. We had recently added a small recreation room overlooking the pool and golf course. This home was built in the middle forties, but Shirley and I had put quite a lot of sweat equity into it. We had ownership from 1972 until 1979, and during that time real estate values had been rising steeply in California.

We were surprised to find out that it had risen nearly five times what we had paid for it, less the cost of the remodeling. We thought that if we could sell the home at current real estate values, we would be able to complete the transaction in Arkansas. All we needed was the right buyer to come along within our time limitation.

During this time there was a home improvement store called Angel's. We went there to purchase some flowers to brighten up the entry for presentation. While there, we met a person who was also buying flowers, so we had an opportunity to tell them about our experience in Arkansas. To our amazement they said they were Christians and referred us to their realtor, who was also a Christian.

It just so happened that this realtor had a friend in the real estate business who was looking for a home. When the friend and his wife saw our house on the golf course and the newly remodeled kitchen and recreation room, they fell in love with it. We closed on the house just in time to meet the time limits set on our new home-to-be in Arkansas, and we left California with great joy in our hearts and money in the bank.

Prior to leaving, we would visit Dad and Mom who lived close by. They were extremely concerned about what we were doing. They knew that neither of us had a job lined up in Arkansas, and they knew that we were taking on a huge debt. We knew they thought we were not doing the sane thing. I tried to assure Dad that everything would be all right. Then one day while standing in his driveway he looked at me and said, "How will you get along?" That was the first time I felt a separation between Dad and me.

I thought I would be representing our business in Arkansas until Dad could follow later. But now I sensed a deep split in our relationship, while at the same time I was building a relationship with God. I answered him with a firm unwavering reply by saying, "God will provide."

Chapter 2
NEW LIFE IN ARKANSAS

My dad was the best friend I ever had. Everything I knew and had learned about business came from him. As I was a child growing up in Minnesota, he taught me how to rebuild boat engines, cars, and motorcycles. I watched as he made his own in-board boat. I saw him reform the hull of a fiberglass boat as he made steps on the bottom to improve the boat's performance. I saw him form and bend deck planks to perfectly fit the shape of the boat. He taught me how to weld and solder, sand and paint. My brother and I helped as he rebuilt and restored three old houses, including an old cabin in northern Minnesota. We learned some of the basics of plumbing and wiring.

One winter, Dad decided to build a motor scooter. He finished before the lake we were living on began its spring thaw. My friends and I had a ball riding the scooter on the ice and in the snow. Dad also built two iceboats that literally flew down the lake at thrilling speeds.

It was no wonder that as we left for Arkansas, I felt torn between leaving my parents and the new venture that God had in store for us. You might call it blind faith calling, but to us it was very real. It was something we just had to do. We were excited to see what God was going to do.

We moved during the month of November, 1979. We packed the kids into our small Volkswagen Rabbit, while my mother volunteered to drive along in our company's Volvo station wagon. I was going to use the Volvo to call on regional accounts. For the first year, things were looking pretty good. We were thrilled with our new home and new friends. Mom stayed with us for the first two weeks, helping us get settled in. She was a big help since our youngest was only one and a half years old.

From time to time, Dad would stop by while on business trips. I struggled to land any new accounts. On the other hand, I was still searching for land on which to move our small business from California. But I could sense that Dad had lost his drive to move. Every time I would show him a potential parcel or building he would shake his head and say he would think about it, but never came to a decision.

In the meantime, Shirley and I were heavily involved in the study of God's Word. We joined a local Baptist church because we liked the way the pastor was teaching the Bible. He was going verse by verse. We were hungry for all the Word and teaching we could get. The more Word we heard the closer we seemed to God. We had a heartfelt desire to know Him.

We couldn't get enough of the Word.

Nearly two years passed, when suddenly the news came to us that Dad had terminal cancer. He came to visit us one day, and I could feel that he was still very concerned about our future and financial condition. For the past two years, Dad had agreed to pay me past wages that we had accrued. I had volunteered in the early years of the company to work for free. Shirley and I lived off her salary as an occupational therapist at that time. The accrued wages had run out, and we were scraping the bottom of the barrel. We volunteered to watch and care for Grandma Sage. Dad and his brothers chipped in together to pay us for taking care of Grandma. We would have taken care of her for nothing if we could have, but they all insisted on paying us.

I began to wonder where God was. We were busy soaking up everything we could read and learn about God, but it seemed like when it came to finances

He disappeared. We volunteered in the local church and felt we were doing what God had called us to do. In a way, we felt like the children of Israel who were called out of Egypt and wandered in the desert for forty years.

We were being attacked by the devil. In addition to Dad having cancer, which was diagnosed in the spring of 1981, we were under tremendous financial pressure. Fortunately, my family was healthy, but we were getting hit in all directions. The first winter was miserably cold. We got about six inches of snow just a few days after arriving. I wasn't expecting that much snow in northwest Arkansas. I had to buy two wood stoves because the heat pump couldn't keep up with the low temperatures. The heat pumps would freeze up, and when that happened there was no heat in the house. They ran off electricity, which was not always a reliable source. Power lines were often knocked down by winter ice or snow storms, and I spent a lot of time cutting and splitting wood for the wood stoves.

The following summer was one of the hottest on record. It was so dry the limbs of the big oaks began falling to the ground. We planted a beautiful garden in the spring only to watch it dry up and die in the heat of the summer. The only source of water was from the well, because the lake was too far away. Every time we had a thunderstorm our pump would get knocked out and we would have to have the local pump company come out and replace the pump.

As I had mentioned before, we were sitting on sixty-six acres. About ten of those sixty-six acres needed to be mowed. I had purchased the mower the former owner had, but it was getting old and was extremely slow. It only had a thirty-six-inch cut and that made for a long couple of days mowing. I found myself mowing every five to six days in the spring. To make the job go easier, I bought a used Kabota tractor with a five-foot cutting deck.

Another expense we hadn't counted on was that Dad decided he needed the Volvo back at work in California. He had hired a new employee and he needed a company car. So Shirley and I found a used Jeep Wagoneer in very good condition. Due to the heavy snows that first winter, I was very happy to have that Jeep. The expenses kept piling up and our bank account kept going down and down. But Shirley and I were so happy we hardly noticed. We had peace and were sure God would pull us out of the predicament we had gotten ourselves into.

In the winter of 1982, Grandma went home to be with the Lord. When she first came into our home, she was a bitter old lady. She was demanding and somewhat sarcastic when she didn't get her own way. Both of us could empathize with her a little. After all, she had been in and out of various nursing homes the past few years. Grandpa had passed away a couple years earlier and Grandma was very alone. In our home it was common practice for us to have an audio tape playing of either Christian music or a preacher preaching. Grandma got an earful of Kenneth Hagin and Kenneth Copeland.

She was raised in the Church of England and held onto her religious beliefs.

But one day a few months before she passed away, she asked us who that was preaching. We told her it was a man of faith teaching a faith message.

That night while getting ready for bed, she lay back on her pillow and asked us to pray for her. She asked us to pray for her salvation, and when we were through she asked the Holy Spirit to fill her. And with a deep sigh a holy peace came over her as she closed her eyes for the night.

A few months later we had to put her in a nursing home because we could no longer attend to her physical needs. She had been in that nursing home before and they told us they didn't want her back on account of her attitude.

But we asked that they just try it for a short while. A couple weeks later the director of the nursing home called and spoke with Shirley. She told her that this was not the same woman they had before, and she asked Shirley what made the difference in her demeanor.

Shirley explained how Grandma would listen to the tapes we were playing and how one day she got born again. It was true. Grandma was a completely different person after she was born again and filled with the Spirit of God.

She was a kinder, gentler person and she went home to be with the Lord in complete peace.

Two months later, in March of 1982, my dad died from melanoma cancer. I had word from my mother that Dad was in the hospital. I told her I would catch the first plane back to California but she told me not to come. She said she would let me know when the right time to come would be. In the meantime, my brother who had been living in Plano, Texas had already arrived in California. I wondered why my brother was told to come and I was told not to come. I knew my mother was completely put off by our love for God. but I didn't know that she had sinister motives.

During the twelve years I worked with Dad, I purchased some company stock. In addition, Dad told me that he had a will prepared, so that enough of his stock would be transferred to me, and I could have control of the business.

Mom knew this, and I believe she acted in fear by coercing my dad to change his will while he was on his death bed. I did not know this at the time, but my mother had confided in my mother-in-law and told her that she had withheld my dad's pain medication in order to get him to change the will. My mother-in-law shared this with Shirley on one of our visits long after Dad had died.

The phone call came, but it wasn't what I expected. Instead of telling me to come so that I could say goodbye to my dad, it was my brother telling me that Dad had passed away. I was devastated to hear the news. I wanted to speak to his bones and tell him to rise up, but I was not at that stage in my faith walk. I got on the next flight from Tulsa to L.A. and pondered all that had happened. I knew that something good was going to happen, but I didn't know what or when.

I arrived in California only to find that there was nothing I could do or say.

Mom was in control. She had her attorney read the will amongst all the relatives present. To my shock, she had taken control of the business. My brother was given Dad's car and my sister received a life insurance policy. I received Dad's watch, a pocketknife, and a pair of shoes. Mom fired me and told me I wasn't needed any more. She said my brother would now be the vice president of the company.

Needless to say, I was deeply hurt. I couldn't understand how my dad could have written me out of his will. But I didn't say anything. I only wondered what would happen next. I was no longer associated with the company and as far as my mom was concerned, she didn't want anything to do with us or my children. That was what I was feeling but in reality, I knew she was afraid of her future. She didn't know how to run the business and now she was alone. She grabbed all she could while she could.

I came home with the pair of shoes which were way too big for me, a Timex watch, and a pocketknife. I told Shirley what had happened, and we both felt the pains my mother must have been going through. I made it priority to forgive her for what she had done. As far as I was concerned it never happened. I began praying for her and for her company. I asked God to bless it and to bless her.

As for Shirley and me, the strings to our financial support were completely cut. We were on our own. For a while I felt like all the faith I had went right out my feet. The devil was doing a good job of stealing from us and putting us in fear. But now we were right where God wanted us, in His hands.

From 1979 until 1982, while we were living on Beaver Lake in the home the Lord had led us to, we had spent a great deal of time reading the Bible. We knew that God's plan for us was to give us a hope and to bless us. We knew that the tests and trials were not from Him. We knew that we were being prepared for something special, but neither of us knew what that would be.

Prior to moving to Arkansas, I was involved in a traffic accident in Reseda, California. One day, Dad and I decided to we would leave work early and drive out to the airport. We had some cleaning to do on an old Twin Beech aircraft we had purchased. While stopped at a traffic light behind another car, a man driving a large sedan came up from behind and slammed into us.

He hit us doing about forty miles an hour. The impact drove us into the car ahead of us and pushed both cars into the intersection. The front seat where. Dad and I were sitting broke down.

As a result of the accident, I had continuous back problems. Dad was also hurt, but he didn't have the lingering pain I was feeling. This accident happened prior to my born-again experience and I was not opposed to getting an attorney to sue for damages. I felt the pain for five years. During that time my back would begin to ache when I would stand for longer than ten minutes, and it would ache when I sat for longer than ten minutes. It prevented me from doing many things. It bothered me constantly, so Dad and I hired an attorney.

One day I took my Volkswagen Rabbit to town in Rogers, Arkansas. Shirley and I decided we would visit the local ice cream shop. While in the store we noticed a bookstand and upon that stand was a book called *I Believe in*

Visions by Kenneth Hagin. At that time, we were still attending the local Baptist church and were still very hungry for God's Word. The title of the book caught my attention, so I purchased it and took it home. I was thrilled to find someone else who had experienced a vision. In fact, from that book I learned that there was a whole new dimension to God that we were missing.

I learned that the vision I had was called an "open vision." I also learned that God was in the healing business. Kenneth Hagin had a marvelous healing ministry and had written many other books on the subject. By reading his books, I began to have faith that God might heal me, too. Then one day while reading the Bible, I saw where God expected us to forgive others that He might in turn forgive us. I thought, maybe if I forgive the man who hit me perhaps God would heal me. I thought I would be a happier person being healed by God than living out the rest of my life in pain. I thought about the driver who had hit us and how for the past five years, he had to think about the lawsuit pending against him. In our tight financial condition, I knew I could use the money, but it now was apparent to me that obeying God's Word was more important. So I picked up the phone and called my attorney in California. I told him I wanted to drop the lawsuit.

The settlement from the lawsuit could have paid off

our home, which was our only debt at the time. It would have also given us money to live on until I found what it was God had called us to Arkansas to do. The attorney was speechless for a moment and then asked why I would want to do such a thing. I told him I had been reading in the Bible where the disciples of Jesus had asked Him to teach them how to pray. And after teaching them the Lord's Prayer, He told them to forgive others so that they in turn could be forgiven by their Heavenly Father.

Again he hesitated and then said, "I take it you found religion?"

I said, "No,

I found Jesus Christ and I believe that if I forgive this man the Lord will heal me." He said he would take me off the lawsuit, and I thanked him for it.

I found out later that the man who hit us had actually been in two accidents that day. He was a drug user. As for me, I was happy to have forgiven him, and I had a great anticipation that God was going to heal me.

Shirley and I had been attending Friday night meetings at homes of various fellow Christians. Each week a new pastor was invited to come and share the Word with us. A week after forgiving this driver, we attended a meeting in the basement of a friend. A pastor, Tom Underhill from

Russelville, Arkansas came and shared the word that God had put on his heart to share.

To be honest, I do not remember a word he said. I was too focused on getting healed. I was thinking and praying that the Holy Spirit would move on him at the end of his message. In fact, I was expecting to get healed. I knew that God's eyes went throughout the earth seeking to whom He can show Himself strong. and I knew He watched over His Word. I had been obedient, and I was expecting.

The moment came. Pastor Underhill finished and the crowd of about seventy-five people began to get up, but suddenly he said, "Wait a minute, wait a minute, the Holy Spirit is saying something to me."

Boy, don't you know that got my complete attention. I was jumping inside. He said, "There is someone in this room who has inflammation of the spinal column and if that person will stand up the Lord will heal you."

Wow, there it was just as I had hoped. I looked around the room to see if there might be someone else standing up. I didn't know what the problem with my back was. In fact, the doctors had taken many x-rays and couldn't find anything wrong. It made me feel like a charlatan, but I knew I was suffering from something. Only God would have known I had an inflamed spinal column. And only a man in tune with the Holy Spirit would have known.

No other person was standing. I jumped up to receive my healing. The pastor came to the middle of the room where I was standing and laid his hand on my forehead. The instant his hand touched me I felt a warm electrical current flow from my head to my feet. I also felt a soothing sensation as the pain left. I began to shout and praise God for His grace and mercy. Everyone in the room could tell that I had received something good from God.

Previously I was not able to pick up my children and hold them or carry them for any period of time. Immediately following my healing, I picked up both of my children and ran up the stairs and down the street, shouting and praising God for what He had done.

That happened in the Fall of 1980, nearly twenty-six years ago, and I have not had any back problems since, except for one little incident. The next morning as I walked into the kitchen I felt a twinge of pain. I had been reading enough of Kenneth Hagin's books to know that this was an attack of the devil. I slapped my hand up against my back and I commanded the devil to take his hands off and never come back again. I shouldn't have been surprised, but I was. The pain left immediately and has never returned.

Although the devil had been stealing from us, our faith

was growing by leaps and bounds. Jesus had said that He had come that we would have life more abundantly. He also said that the devil came to steal and to kill. We were beginning to see how the devil had been working in our lives. We also were seeing how God was working.

The devil wasn't through with us. He had several more ways in which he could defeat us financially. After Dad died, I had the company's video camera and I thought I could start a video company. I was going to offer its services to the local real estate companies. Many of the properties that were listed by these realtors were located out in the country. It took many man hours to drive a prospective buyer out to see them. I thought they could show the customer a video first and save the trip if he didn't like what he saw on the video.

I had cards and flyers printed. We had no income, so we sold one of our cars and sold many of our precious household items at a flea market. One day, not too long after I started the business and not too long after Dad died, I had a knock at the door. It was my brother Bob from Texas. I was very happy to see him, but I could tell by the look on his face that he was not happy about coming. He told me that Mom had asked him to come and get the video equipment that belonged to the company. I was shocked but had no recourse other than to give it to him. He said he was really sorry. I knew he meant it from the bottom of his heart.

About a year earlier, before Dad came down with cancer, Bob and I took a trip to Chicago together. We were going to the National Restaurant Show where we would also meet Dad. Bob drove up from Plano, Texas and picked me up at our home on Beaver Lake. Prior to his coming, Shirley and I

were in prayer many days asking God to give us an opportunity to share Jesus Christ with Bob. That evening after he arrived, we had dinner and following that I asked Bob if I could share something with him. He knew what was coming, because he knew why we left California and why we were in Arkansas. He was fully aware of our zeal for God.

For the next hour I shared God's plan of salvation. I told him why it was necessary for God to send Jesus and why man needed a Savior. I then askedhim if he would like to ask Jesus into his heart. He said, "Yes." That evening brother Bob was born again. We all celebrated.

The next day we left for Chicago. On the way, I noticed that the air in the car had a strange odor. I had forgotten that as a young boy in Minnesota, Bob had frozen his feet. He played outside in the winter too long without his boots on, and for the next thirty-five years he suffered with a serious foot odor. When we arrived in Chicago I shared a motel room with him.

When we were in the room it was necessary to keep the door and window open. After the show, we began our trip home and spent a night in Springfield, Illinois. While in the motel I felt compassion for my brother's foot problem, so I pulled out the Bible in the nightstand drawer. I told Bob that God wanted to heal his feet. I shared how Jesus went about doing good and healing all who were oppressed by the devil, for God was with Him.

I opened the Bible to James 5:14-17 and read that scripture to him. I told Bob that if we anointed his feet with oil God would heal them, and I asked him if he believed God's Word. He said he did. So I went off to the bathroom to find some oil. I found some Vitalis hair oil and brought it back to Bob. I then anointed his feet with the Vitalis and prayed that God would heal them. About three months later, Bob was on another trip and he stopped by our home and told me God had healed his feet. He was so emphatic about it he held up his sweaty cowboy boot and stuffed it into my nose. Sure enough, there was absolutely no odor. We praised God together.

I knew Bob was reluctant about having to pick up the video camera. Mom wanted it back so that she could sell it. She was dealing with the IRS and attorneys and needed every cent she could find. She was afraid, and neither Shirley nor I could fault her. We continued to pray for her and asked God to bless her.

Shortly thereafter, we listed our home with a local realtor. Due to my healing experience I realized that it was God's plan to heal anyone who would come to Him. I saw what happened with my brother and shared it with other friends. It wasn't long before Shirley and I were seeking the baptism in the Holy Spirit. We had heard of the baptism by the Holy Spirit into the body of Christ and the baptism in water but we were not familiar with the baptism in the Holy Spirit with the evidence in speaking in tongues.

One day while attending another one of those Friday night meetings, a young lady was speaking on the baptism of the Holy Spirit. At the end of the meeting, Shirley and I went forward to be prayed for. When Shirley was prayed for, she immediately began speaking in tongues. It was flowing so rapidly out of her mouth I stood in amazement. Later she said it felt like she had hot coals on her lips. I knew she had received from God, and I wanted to receive also. But when she laid hands on me, I did not have the utterance like Shirley. Only one word came forth. I went home a little disappointed.

Weeks later, Shirley had arisen early to pray. She came back to the bedroom to tell me that God told her that I was baptized in the Holy Spirit and that I needed to speak the word I was given in faith. So I began saying that one word over and over. To my surprise, God added another word and then another. Within a week I was speaking sentences and within a month it flowed without limitation. The Apostle Paul told his church that he spoke in tongues more than them all. He said that he desired that they speak in tongues. To me, that was a command from God, not an option. Jesus said that His disciples would speak in tongues. I wanted everything God had, and I wasn't going to let religious tradition rob God's Word of its power.

Shortly after receiving the baptism of the Holy Spirit, I was listening to Kenneth Copeland telling a story about how speaking in tongues builds your faith and how power comes upon you. He said that after praying in tongues all day he went to a meeting, and upon laying his hand on a man needing prayer the fellow flew off the chair he was sitting in. I thought I would try praying in tongues all day long and see what happened. That evening, I had a call from a friend who had been in bed with a migraine headache for four days. He asked me if I would come and pray for him.

I called another friend who I knew also prayed and spoke in tongues. I asked him if he would come along. When we arrived at the house we found the man with the headache in bed. I asked him to stand up so that we could pray for him. As I lay my hand on his shoulder he would cry out in pain. I asked him what was happening and he said when I lay my hand on his right shoulder the pain would jump to his left shoulder. And when I lay my hand on his left shoulder the pain would jump to the right shoulder. My friend and I rebuked the devil and commanded the pain to leave in Jesus name. I told the man in bed to take a walk and to praise God for healing him. I called him the next day and he had gone to the hospital to visit another sick person. His son said that his dad was just fine. Kenneth Copeland was right, because he was teaching God's Word that says that you will be filled with power after the Holy Spirit comes upon you.

In those early years of testing, we learned that giving was better then receiving. However, financially we were not exactly reaping a harvest. We were giving to the church and to others who had a need. One such fellow was a man we met as he was walking down the long road that led out to our home on Beaver Lake. We stopped to offer him a ride. Along the way he began to tell us that he had been laid off from his job at a local trucking company. We drove him to his home, which we found out was a trailer sitting close to the lake down a rocky dirt road. For our kindness, he invited us to come and have dinner with him and his family, a wife and two boys.

During our course of conversation, we further learned that they were flat broke. They had a large propane tank sitting outside that was empty and the local gas company would not fill it up since they owed money on the last refill.

Shirley and I were amazed at this guy's hospitality. We wondered how he could afford to feed two more people. He prepared a delicious chicken dinner, as he loved to cook and entertain. We went home that evening wondering how they were going to make it through the rest of the winter without propane. They needed it for heating, cooking, and hot water. We thought about his young children and wife being alone at home without those amenities. He was looking for odd jobs since he had carpentry skills, but it had been a while since his last job and there was little hope he would be called back to work at the trucking firm.

The next day I arose and drove down to the gas company. I paid off their old bill and paid for a refill of their tank. That got them through the winter, and Shirley and I were happy we could help out our new friends. We didn't tell them what we had done, but it wasn't hard for him to figure it out.

One day our new friend came over to ask if he could borrow our car. I was hesitant, since I had spent several days detailing our recently purchased Jeep Wagoneer. I didn't even know if he had a driver's license or insurance, but because the Bible says to lend to those who ask I readily told him to take it. I didn't know that this was not going to be for just a day.

He asked if he could borrow it longer, so I told him to go ahead. I also told him to take it for the week if he needed it. Well, a week ran into nearly six months.

During that time, he managed to get stuck on a tree stump and bend the rear bumper. Then one day in the early fall I heard a knock on the door and I saw him standing there. He said, "I have bad news; I was coming down your driveway and somehow as I was making the turn the car slipped in the freshly fallen snow and slid off the road. It's okay; it's resting on its side against a tree." After that I asked him to find other transportation which he willingly did.

Shortly after that experience I sold the Jeep. I used the money to buy the Kabota tractor. Since the Bible says to give and it shall be given unto you, it wasn't long before we had a new car given to us. We had been using our small Volkswagen Rabbit as our sole source of transportation after selling the Jeep. It was tight accommodations for Grandma, my wife, my two children and me. When the five of us arrived at Dad's cabin in Northern Minnesota in our Rabbit with our clothes in paper bags, he decided to buy us a car. I knew this was a real stretch for Dad and really appreciated his kindness and generosity.

In the spring of 1982, we lived off the proceeds we received from the sale of that car. We also listed our home for sale. Several months passed before we had an offer on the house. We had been praying that God would send a buyer. The first offer came from a man who offered us a price well below the market value and well below what I had paid for the property in 1979.

I told the realtor that I could not accept the offer. I told him that I was a Christian and I believed that God had a better offer for us. I was desperate to sell the house, but I had faith to believe for a better offer.

Shirley and I were concerned that we wouldn't be able to make the house payments. So we prayed and asked God to give us favor with the seller from whom we purchased the house. I went to him and explained our situation and asked him if he would wait until the house sold. He said he was not in any hurry for the funds and that he would be happy to work with us. Shirley and I rejoiced at his response. If he had foreclosed on the loan, we could have lost all the equity we had in that house. It was the equity that later helped us start the business that God had planned for us.

About a week later, we had another offer on the house. Another realtor, a Christian, had seen our house listed in the multiple listing guide and decided to show it to his customer. When I was introduced to the man, I sensed that God was telling me that he was the person who was going to buy the property. I did not say anything to him at that time, but later after we had closed on the sale I told him what God had said to me that day we met. I was shocked at his response. He said, "He spoke to you?"

"Yes" I responded.

He said, "God woke me up in the middle of the night. It was three o'clock in the morning and told me to buy this property!" Whew, I didn't know he was also a Christian and therefore my words were not taken in offense. Instead, he knew God and knew that I had told him the truth. This man made an offer close to our asking price. This gave us a fair profit. He wanted to pay cash with part down and the balance in January of 1983.

This was a much better deal than our first offer and I knew God was watching over my words. His down payment met our living expenses until the closing. We had to budget, but we made it. In the meantime, I was desperate to know what God wanted me to do. I was torn between preaching, going into real estate, or going into manufacturing. I took a real estate course and got my license for the state of Arkansas. But I was not happy about real estate, and I realized that I was not called to be a preacher.

On the other hand, I loved manufacturing. I loved working with my dad building machines that were used to clean restaurants, supermarkets, schools and hospitals. I loved the manufacturing part, but I did not love the cleaning side of the business. I had learned bookkeeping, accounting, purchasing, manufacturing, quality control, boxing, shipping, marketing, and sales. In fact, when I left Dad's business I was the vice president. That meant I could clean the restrooms, paint the halls and do all the jobs no one else would do.

One night after asking God's direction about whether I should go into manufacturing or real estate, I had a dream. In that dream I found myself walking down a staircase in a large hotel. As I descended, I saw a beautiful blonde woman sitting in the stairwell. She was wearing a fur coat. I wondered what she was doing there. As I approached her to pass by, she suddenly opened up her coat. She was naked to the waist. But what shocked me was that from the waist down she had the body of a dog. I was repulsed and woke up in shock. I sat straight up in bed with my eyes wide open. I had never had such a dream before. In the morning, I asked God to show me what the dream meant.

I had my real estate license hanging on the wall of a local realtor. In the morning I went to his office. He asked me to take a listing down to the local multiple listing office. When I arrived, a beautiful blonde came to the counter to receive the information. Instantly I recognized her as being the person I had seen the night before in my dream. The only conclusion I could come to was that for me real estate was taboo. God wanted me in manufacturing.

When we had received the baptism of the Holy Spirit with evidence of speaking in tongues, we began a search for a new church. We found one called Ozark Word Church, which was just starting. One of the visions of the pastor was to have satellite broadcasts of well-known full gospel preachers.

On one of those occasions there was a pastor from England, Arkansas by the name of Charles Capps. In his message, he said that there would be believers who would come up with "new and witty inventions." I said to myself and to God that that was me. He prophesied it and I received it! The only thing was I did not know at the time what it would be.

The Bible says that as a man plans his ways the Lord

will direct his steps.

My steps from the moment we left California until this time were certainly unusual to me. God was leading me in dreams and visions. Now God was about to spring a whole new life upon us. It would be a life filled with blessing and abundance.

It was while I was attending this same church that my dad died. When he died I was comforted by my friends. The devil had me standing in fear the first week after my dad's death. The only thing I knew was his support and all the lessons he had taught me. And at that moment I felt very alone and weak.

I told one of my Christian friends how I felt, and he recognized that fear wasn't from God. He asked me if he could pray for me. Immediately he rebuked the fear and it left. I was shaking and the shaking stopped. From that time forward, I began to earnestly consider manufacturing.

I had an idea floating through my head. When Grandma was staying with us, it was difficult to take her shopping. She was physically unable to walk or get around. But every time Shirley would leave her at home she would get very upset and become very sarcastic. Many times, we would bring her along and use a wheelchair. But even the wheelchair was a chore to get into the car.

It wasn't until after Grandma passed away that I began to seriously think about manufacturing an electric shopping cart. I thought people like my grandma could use them in the grocery stores. It was this idea that won out over my desire for real estate and going into the ministry. I thought that such a product could help millions of people all over the world. The only thing was I had never seen a commercial cart. I had seen personal carts, but not a commercial cart.

Chapter 3
A NEW BEGINNING

On January 1, 1983, I was determined to begin manufacturing a commercialelectric shopping cart. I thought I had been sitting around long enough waiting for God to show me what to do. But in my head and my heart He had already begun the process. I began by purchasing some tools. I went to the local iron yard and purchased some square tubing. In about four months I had completed the first shopping cart.

Shirley decided to give it a name. She came up with Mart Cart™. And that was the beginning of a whole new industry of electric shopping carts that would enter the grocery store environment. I prayed while I worked and was very pleased with the way it came out. I liked the yellow fiberglass bodies and the strong steel frame.

I needed a salesman, so I hired that fellow who borrowed my car. He was a natural salesman. He a special gift of making friends with everyone he met. He pioneered these sales. He turned over every rock. I paid him a commission on every unit he sold. He told me that at one time he used to work in a grocery store. He told the manager that someday he would see electric shopping carts rolling down the aisle! Was that prophesy? How interesting that he would be selling an electric shopping cart to grocery stores.

Before coming to work for me, he had been rehired at the trucking company he used to work for, so he had purchased a new pickup truck. He offered to use it take the cart to the national supermarket show that was being held in Chicago. I had designed a brochure and had it printed. It came off the press around the first of May 1983. The show was a few days later. I told him that he needed to read and study that brochure and then use that knowledge to sell the carts. He was eager to learn and couldn't wait to begin selling.

It was no surprise that there was no competition at the show. I thought we would sell a hundred or more. But that was not to be. People were very mean-spirited. Some told us they didn't want that kind of people in their store.

They were referring to little old ladies. Others told us they didn't want their stock boys racing up and down the aisles. And then some told us they didn't want the liability nor the expense. Many couldn't see the need, except one couple from East Windsor, Connecticut. They purchased two carts. They had several elderly people who came to their store every week.

They just couldn't make it around the store without having to take a breather. This wonderful couple purchased a large ad in the local newspaper advertising the fact that they had a new electric cart for so and so and so and so. They actually named their customers and invited them to come in and use the new carts. The newspaper covered the front page of the business section with a story about the new service Chester's Market was providing.

Chester's Market sent us a copy of the newspaper ad and the front page of the business section. We used that writeup to convince local grocery stores that they needed to serve their customers by providing them a lift. The title of the article was, "Wheels of Progress Roll Down Grocery Aisles." Below the title was a picture of an elderly lady on the cart. Slowly, we began to sell carts to grocery stores around Northwest Arkansas.

It became apparent that users of the carts were not just the elderly. We found out that people with all types of mobility limitations were using them. We also found out that if we put just one cart in a store people wouldn't use it.

The reason eluded us at first, but when we asked certain people why they weren't using it they would tell us that they felt they needed to leave it for a person with greater limitations than they had. Some people were offended by it and would simply let their pride keep them from using it.

We were selling several hundred carts a year in our fourth year of manufacturing. By this time, Shirley and I were happy to have a business that was prospering. We were able to at least put groceries in the refrigerator and pay all our bills. It looked like things were going well, but we hadn't landed chain stores. All of our sales were to mom and pop grocery stores. Their owners were concerned about competition with the big stores and saw a way to gain more customers. They also saw that their customers would buy more groceries because they would spend more time in the store.

The Mart Cart™ was a win win win situation for all concerned. The store was blessed, the user was blessed, and we were blessed.

Then the old devil raised his head again, but God had an answer every time.

Shortly after beginning my manufacturing company, I hired an accountant to do my tax return. What I failed to consider was the profit we had made on the sale of our home. I was counting on using that profit to start and run our business. Fortunately, or unfortunately as the case may be, he found it and reported it on our tax return. Our bank account took a big hit when we paid the taxes due.

In rapid succession, we suddenly had a notice from

the bank that we owed them $25,000. Several years earlier Dad and I had purchased a plane. I was a joint partner with my dad. When Dad died, my mom demanded possession of the airplane. The plane was based at the Van Nuys, California airport, so I gladly told her to do whatever she wanted to with it. She wanted to sell it and I couldn't have agreed more. From where I was in Arkansas, I didn't feel I could handle the sale any better than she could.

Apparently, I was wrong. Mom sold it to a man who claimed to be an owner of several prosperous businesses. Mom worked out a deal where he was to pay off the balance with the bank. The man agreed, but did not make any payments. Instead, he sold the plane to a couple of unsuspecting men from South America.

When we received the notice from the bank, we were in shock. We thought the plane had been sold and paid for. We discussed the mess with our pastor at Ozark Word Church because he happened to be an airplane dealer. He said, "Give me the identification number and I will find the airplane." We were greatly relieved and amazed that God had put someone with knowledge of airplanes in our midst.

Our pastor got on a plane and flew to California to find our lost airplane. He checked with some local airports and found out that the plane had been flying out of Chino, a small airport in Southern California.

He went to the airport and learned that the plane was often used on night flights to South America. He thought the men who had the airplane could possibly be dealing drugs. He notified the local police, who in turn notified the DEA.

They set up a trap to catch the men as they arrived early in the morning. Cars were lined up on the tarmac with dogs and police waiting for them as they taxied up to their hanger. As the men got out of the airplane, they were taken by surprise. But the real surprise was they were bona fide businessmen.

Our pastor told us that they were dealing in leather goods and had purchased the airplane from the guy Mom had sold it to. They had even gone as far as to recondition the airplane by installing new engines. Our pastor told them that he represented the true owner who had the title at the bank. He let them know that if they wanted clear title, they would have to pay the bank the balance that I owed. The businessmen wrote our pastor a check, who deposited it with the bank. We were deeply grateful for what our pastor did for us.

God had used our pastor to help us out of tough spot, but there was another problem already raising its head. It was a problem that began to show itself shortly after I began manufacturing. It was a problem that actually began when I was about ten years old, and was steadily getting worse. It worked so slowly on my body that I didn't know what was happening. I began to get very tired and could barely finish a day's production. I was wearing all the hats and doing all the work for the first year. That meant many hours standing on my feet during the manufacturing process. For a healthy person it probably wouldn't have been a big deal.

I began to complain to Shirley that I was feeling weak and tired. I noticed that my ears would have a ringing sound and my gums were tender and bled easily. There were many other symptoms such as weakness in the legs. I remember that it got so bad I couldn't walk from the basement door to he front door of our split-level home. I went to the doctor and he diagnosed it as chronic fatigue syndrome. My legs felt like I had multiple sclerosis.

All the while I was dealing with these symptoms, I was trying to build and run a manufacturing company.

Then one day a friend of ours sent us a copy of an article in a local paper describing the effects of mercury poisoning. The article mentioned the name of a doctor in Springdale, Arkansas who specialized in disorders similar to what I had. Springdale is a town very close to Rogers.

I was very happy to have received that article, because it described almost every symptom I was having. I made an appointment to see the doctor.

He ran a blood test and a skin test. He told me that out of a thousand patients, my reaction to the skin test was the worst he had ever seen. My body was showing a severe reaction to the mercury used in the filings in my teeth.

I was extremely allergic to mercury. He suggested that I have the mercury removed as soon as possible. I did as he said, but it took the next twenty years in order for me to regain my strength. It came back to me about as slowly as the effects of the mercury penetrated my body.

When I was about ten years old, I began speed skating. A local neighbor had encouraged me to try it. He had two sons, Vince and Vance, who were very good at it. I had a very illustrious career by winning the Minnesota Ten Thousand Lakes championship and later the Canadian Championship. But now as I look back on sports in my youth, I can see how mercury robbed me of my strength. At the time I did not associate the filings with the weakness I often felt. I eventually gave up speed skating due to my lack of energy. It seemed as a youth there was never any lack of energy until my encounter with mercury.

Despite the setbacks with the airplane, the bank, the tax

return and the mercury poisoning, our business continued to grow. Eventually we began to sell into the large chains. But that too came with great pains. For the first four years, we were without any competition. We would take our carts to the largest supermarket convention in the United States. That convention was called FMI for Food Market Institute.

In our fourth year at FMI, a competitor showed up from Canada. They offered their carts at a price that was half the cost of mine. We had been trying to get into the chain stores, but they weren't convinced that the cost was worth the investment. But when our competitor showed up with two carts for the price of one, the chains bit. Some purchased a large quantity of carts from the Canadian manufacturer.

To see those chains purchase carts from another supplier after we had spent four years of hard work and a great deal of money trying to sell them ours was a big blow. It seemed like every extra dollar we could afford I would put into printed material for mailings or would put my salesman on an airplane to go see those chains. I remember complaining to God asking why we didn't get the orders. There were about four major chains that purchased from our new competitor. They bought about twenty-five carts at a time. To us, that would have amounted to about two to three months of sales at that time.

Fortunately, business didn't stop. Having competition only reinforced the concept of the value electric shopping carts added to the grocery store. I knew we had a better a cart, because it was designed for heavy usage. It was a commercial cart, not a home cart. In a few months we began to get calls asking us if we had parts for our competitor's carts. The chains were having great difficulty getting service, as well as parts. One thing we learned early on was that once a grocery store started using a cart they demanded immediate service when it failed. They did not want an unhappy customer.

Within a year, all the chains that had purchased from our competitor began to purchase carts from us. The old adage "you get what you pay for" certainly came into play in this instance. As a result of that experience, we have been able to maintain nearly seventy percent or more of the market for electric shopping carts.

Today we sell over nine thousand carts a year in a world-wide market. This number is still growing annually, due to a marvelous invention that has made our carts more affordable and less expensive to maintain. Several years ago, I became intrigued by hub motors. Back then they called them pancake motors because they were flat. They became popular on electric bicycles.

I had wanted a cart that had a zero turning radius. To

achieve this, I could either use a differential drive system, which was costly, or I could use a front wheel drive motor. Before the hub motor, the only choice was a right angle drive motor, which also was very costly to make. The hub motor would be the perfect answer if we could get it to work at the slow speed we needed.

All the hub motor manufactures said they couldn't make them work in the speed and torque range we needed. We knew the stakes were high, because ifwe could achieve our goals we would be able to manufacture a cart with better performance and longer life than our competitors.

Once again, I know it was by divine grace that we had on our staff an employee who was a genius when it came to working with gears. He began looking into the hub motor concept and made it his challenge to prove the motor manufacturers wrong. In perhaps a year and half, he not only had designed a hub motor that would work, but one that was beyond our expectations. We found under testing that simulated a three hundred pound rider, the motor lasted three times longer than the motor we had been using. And that was saying a lot, because the motor we were using was one of the best in the industry.

The marvel of a hub motor is that it does not require any belts, chains, or pulleys. This reduces cost and simplifies service in the field. This is what has made our Mart

Cart XTi so popular with grocery stores. In addition, we achieved the zero turning radius, making the carts extremely maneuverable in narrow grocery aisles. To back up our new motor, we offered the best warranty in the industry.

When I first began making electric shopping carts, I started in my garage.

As you know, Shirley and I had sold our home on Beaver Lake and moved into a much smaller home in Rogers, Arkansas. For the first nine months, I built, sold, and shipped carts out of that garage. But as the sales increased it was necessary to find larger manufacturing space.

Rogers did not have much to offer at that time, so I ended up renting about 1,200 square feet in Prairie Creek. It was a two-car garage with a small office located behind a small strip mall. For the next year, I manufactured carts in that building, and it was there that I hired my first full time employee. He told me no one would hire him because he had been in a terrible car accident that messed up his back. What I heard was honesty and what I saw was a young man that I believed could do the work. He is still with our company today and has done a marvelous job.

In 1985, we moved from Prairie Creek to a small warehouse in Avoca, Arkansas. It was a dusty, dirty place because it wasn't insulated or sealed well, but it offered us about six thousand square feet of affordable space.

While here, I remember telling God that if He wanted this business to continue to grow, I was going to need a lot of money to make it happen.

In fact, I thought it would take about $25,000 to purchase all the desks, conveyors, and other equipment I needed. I had laid out a long list of items I needed in front of Him. It wasn't long after that when I had a thought pass through my mind to call Wal-Mart to see if they had any used conveyors they would like to sell. The warehouse manager I spoke to told me that I had called at the right time, because they had just moved in tons of conveyors.

They were remodeling their stores, and all of the old conveyors had to go. So they arranged to have them shipped into their obsolete number one store in

Rogers.

I dropped what I was doing and ran down to their old store. Inside I found stacks and stacks of beautiful used conveyors. There must have been several thousand feet of conveyors. I called the manager back and told him I would like to purchase about one hundred feet of their heavy-duty used conveyors.

He told me that would cost about five thousand dollars. Since I didn't have that kind of money at that time I told him I would have to think about it.

The next day I decided that his offer wasn't too bad a deal, so I went back into the old store again to look for some I could use. Upon entering, I saw another man walking around inside. I stopped him and asked him if he was there to buy conveyors also. He said he was from the local iron scrap yard and that he had come to bid on the metal. I asked him what it would be worth and he

told me about five cents a pound! I rushed back to my office and called the manager again and told him about the conversation I had with the other man.

I told him I would offer twice the amount he was willing to pay. There was silence on the other end of the phone and then he asked how many feet I needed. I began to think about the future and how much more I could use to meet future growth. I told him I needed three hundred feet. He said, "Pick out what you need and write Wal-Mart a check for $1,000.00."

It turned out to be a win win situation for both of us. I could have easily spent thousands of dollars more. As things turned out, I was able to give some conveyor to a friend who needed it for his manufacturing business.

Not too long after I purchased the conveyor, I received a phone call from my brother Bob. He called to ask me if

I needed any desks. I told him that at the moment I didn't, but I had hopes that the business would continue to grow, and if it did I would certainly need some. He told me Phillips Petroleum was closing a local office and they were having an auction on all their furnishings. I went to the auction and was able to purchase about thirty desks for between thirty and fifty dollars each. Many were Steelcase desks that had beautiful laminate tops and steel drawers. These would normally sell for six hundred to nine hundred dollars. I could see that God had once again heard my prayers and He was making provision for our next expansion.

It didn't take long and we were looking for another building. Although we had only been in that dusty old warehouse a few months, I began been looking for a new building. I was praying about that, too. One day I had a call from a realtor who asked me if I needed a building. I hadn't told anyone that I was looking, but somehow he had heard about our business. He told me he had a metal building for sale. It was something that he had just listed. He told me they wanted a quick sale because they were going out of business.

The two of us went to look at the building. It was nearly new and in beautiful condition. It had about twenty-four hundred feet of office space and about sixteen thousand square feet of usable warehouse and manufacturing space. And it was available below the appraised value!

I signed the papers and we moved in.

It was in August of 1987 when we began our move. About that time I had a call from my mother, who said she had made a mistake taking over

Dad's business. She said she wanted to sell it. She said that she should never have taken on that responsibility. I told her I was interested. We made a gentleman's agreement over the phone. My brother had been acting as vice president from his home in Plano, Texas. He had called me several times earlier to tell me that things were not going well between him and Mom, and he wanted me to buy Mom out. Mom had also confided in me that she was not pleased with the amount of money Bob was making.

Mom and I agreed to meet together at a trade show in Texas. I told her I would build new machines for her, because the equipment she was manufacturing was outdated. They were designed nearly twenty years earlier. There had been some significant improvements in the components, which she had not incorporated. We were to meet and work out the details of the sale at the show.

I spent a couple of months gathering information from suppliers in the spray cleaning industry. I had several salesmen bring in their samples of new pumps, guns, unloaders, and other components. By the time the show came

I had developed two new machines. I was confident she would like what she saw and couldn't wait to meet her. I accomplished this feat in the midst of a move to our new facility and while contending with the mercury poisoning.

I called Mom and told her I had the new machines completed and that I looked forward to seeing her in Texas.

We met at the show, and she agreed to complete the sale. She mailed me her stock certificates so that I could have an attorney complete the paperwork.

I remember the stock arrived on Friday afternoon by United Parcel. On the following Sunday, Mom called me and told me she did not want to sell the business to me. After all the work and time I had put into making the new equipment, I was appalled. But I shouldn't have been. I should have known my mom well enough to know that her word was not reliable, based on past experience. Had I been dealing with anyone else I would have had them sign a sales agreement, but being my mom I wanted her to feel that I trusted her.

She eventually sold the business to someone else for a fraction of what I was willing to pay and in the process fired my brother.

I really felt sorry for my brother. The only work he had known was the manufacturing and sales of spray cleaning equipment. In addition, I was sitting with the two new spray cleaners I had designed and parts for a dozen more. I called Bob and asked him if he would like a job. Bob moved to

Northwest Arkansas to begin his new career and Sage Industries had a new division.

Sage Industries was a name Dad had approved when I started a sideline business in California of making and selling an automotive aftermarket product called the Cool Curtain. Dad's business was Sage Systems Inc. When I moved to Arkansas, I used the Sage Industries Inc. name. It was under this name that I made and sold the Mart Carts. I used this name from 1983 when we were incorporated until 1989. In 1989, we were sued by the company which bought Mom's business claiming we were infringing on their trademark. Rather than fight them, I quickly settled the lawsuit by changing our corporate name to Assembled Products™ Corporation. I did this because the Bible says to settle your differences quickly. In the long run, I feel good about my decision but I miss the right to use my own name.

The Bible also tells us that if we commit our ways unto the Lord He will guide our steps. I honestly cannot recall

all the times my steps were ordered of the Lord. I do, however, recall a few more instances.

Assembled Products Corporation continued to grow through the '80s and '90's. During that time, we would either create new products or people would knock on our door and bring us new products. As a result, our sales grew, as well as the number of employees. Now, in 2006, we have approximately one hundred and fifty employees, with sales approaching thirty million dollars a year. Our goal is to exceed one hundred million dollars in gross revenue per year. With the patents, current products, and new products we are developing, I believe we should reach that goal in the near future.

To handle growth in the '90's, we needed more people and space. We had been talking about purchasing one building in which to house all the divisions. That would mean bringing Mart Cart™, Spray Master Technologies™, and Jotto Desk™ under one roof. To accomplish this, we would need about one hundred thousand square feet of manufacturing and warehouse space. It would also mean finding a large piece of property on which to build the facility that would work best for us.

For several years, I mulled the thought around in my head about finding the right piece of property. One day in 1997, I was sitting at my desk when I felt a sudden urge to go look. I knew it was the Lord leading me, so I just followed along. I got in my car and drove directly to the Bentonville airport.

On the west side of the airport there is a long straight road, I Street, that runs north and south and connects two major highways. As I drove up the street. I noticed a twenty-five-acre parcel for sale. I thought this would be absolutely perfect for our needs. I rushed back to the office to inform our vice president. Soon after, he made an offer on the land and it wasn't long after that it became ours.

Now this is what happened to the land. For a while it was our fullest intention to build. In fact, we had even hired an engineering firm to draw up the building plans for large-scale development. Shortly after purchasing the property, the city of Bentonville asked if they could run a sewer line down the front edge of the property. In addition, they offered to pay us for the easement.

A little while later, the city wanted to run a water line and offered to pay us again. The city's improvements added immediate value. But what we hadn't foreseen was the sudden population growth that was to happen over the next ten years. Along with the population growth, property values began to increase rapidly. It was reported that Northwest Arkansas was the eighth fastest growing area in the United States. And as of this writing in April of 2006, it is still growing at a phenomenal rate.

We saw the value of that land rise from the $18,000 we paid per acre to over $120,000. It became very obvious that it was too good of an investment to build a manufacturing facility on. So, we split the land into two twelve-acre parcels. We sold the first section and were able to use the net proceeds for the expansion of our Jotto Desk facilities and on the purchase of other land.

The Lord wanted to bless us and that He did! If we had built the building we had originally designed, we would have been 100,000 square feet short of our present needs. Assembled Products Corporation now utilizes about 167,000 square feet of manufacturing and warehouse space and we are still growing.

I have been relating stories about being led by the Spirit of God. I remember a day about two years ago when I met a friend for lunch. He was very saddened and upset. I asked him what was troubling him, and he told me a very good friend of his was in the hospital. He went on to say that his friend was dying. With a deep sigh he said, "And there is nothing I can do about it."

I felt his pain, but something on the inside of me said, "What do you mean there is nothing you can do about it? Is God dead?" I repeated what I heard to my friend. I then said something along this line: "Didn't Jesus tell us we had authority over all the works of the devil? Didn't He say that greater is He who is in us than he who is in the world? Didn't He command us to go lay hands on the sick, to cast out demons, raise the dead, and heal the lepers? Didn't He say we would be filled with power after the Holy Ghost came upon us? Didn't Jesus Himself go about doing good, healing all who were sick and oppressed of the devil? Didn't He tell us to be followers of Him?" I then asked him if there was anything that would prevent us from going down to the hospital and praying for his friend.

He agreed with what I had said and told me that there wasn't any reason keeping us from going to see his friend. So we finished lunch and went down to the hospital. On the way, we were both praying in the Spirit. By the time we got there we had great expectations that God would intervene on behalf of his friend who was dying.

When we arrived at the hospital, we encountered all of this man's relatives and pastor in the waiting room next to the intensive care ward. It was my understanding that at any moment they would receive word that this man had passed away. But God had different plans that day!

My friend greeted his friend's wife and daughter. They accompanied us into the intensive care room where his friend lay. He was connected to several monitoring units and had been put into a coma by the doctors. Standing at the foot of the bed, I said, "So and so, rise up in the name of Jesus." From our standpoint, that is what we could see with our eyes, nothing had happened.

I knew that in the name of Jesus everything in heaven and earth had to bow, and I expected the disease that was killing this man had to leave.

As my friend continued in silent prayer I said a second time, "So and so, rise up in the name of Jesus." But this time I said it like I really meant it. Again, there was no outward sign of any change. So for a third time I said in a loud commanding voice filled with authority, "So and so, rise up in the name of Jesus."

Suddenly the monitors which had been nearly flatlined sprang to life! His vital signs on the monitor suddenly became alive. His body, on the other hand, showed no sign of improvement. But all of us were thrilled at what the monitors were doing. I said to myself, "Jesus has healed him!" We all left the room. My friend stopped to speak with the pastor, and I continued to the lobby. I had an overwhelming desire to sit down and praise God for the marvelous miracle He had just performed.

It took a couple more months in the hospital before his friend was released.

I know that the work the Lord did in his body that day was all that he needed to survive the days ahead. Now he has fully recovered and is once again living a healthy life.

On another occasion, a relative's wife had been diagnosed with ovarian cancer. She was very upset and concerned about her diagnosis because she had two adorable young children and a wonderful husband to care for. She was a Christian and knew that Shirley and I would often pray for the sick. She asked us to come to the hospital and pray for her. She was familiar with James 5:14, where he told the church to anoint the sick with oil. So we anointed her and prayed for her. When she had further tests done, the report came back stating that the cancer was gone!

As her faith grew, there came a day when she broke a bone in her foot. She went to the doctor and had x-rays taken. A small spur was chipped off the bone of one joint. The doctor said this was a very difficult injury to heal, and if she didn't improve in the next couple of weeks they would have to operate. She came over to our house and asked us to pray again, which we did.

A couple of weeks later her foot was still tender. The doctor performed an operation. What she found was a complete shock to her. She found that the bone had reattached itself and was healing just fine. She told our relative she must know someone special upstairs. The Lord was healing that foot, but sometimes we get impatient and hinder the work He is doing.

The Bible says that those who are led by the Spirit are the sons of God.

It also tells us that God is a spirit and that we must pray in the spirit.

Jesus put it this way: He commanded His disciples to wait for the gift He was sending from His Father, i.e. the Holy Spirit. It was a promised gift, a heavenly gift that he desired His disciples to have. On one occasion He said. "Be filled with the Spirit."

Jesus couldn't have made it more clear. He said He had come to destroy the works of the devil. Be filled with the Spirit. He said He had come so that we could have life more abundantly. Be filled with the Spirit. He told His disciples to do the works He had done. Be filled with the Spirit. He said that after the Holy Spirit had come upon them, they would be filled with authority over all the power of the enemy. He said they would speak in other tongues, and, later, by His Spirit through the apostle Paul. He said, "I desire that you speak in tongues." Tongues is not the issue; obedience is.

Shirley and I have been extremely blessed since we left California. We answered God's call and live daily expecting great things to happen.

Recently, we witnessed one of the most wonderful miracles we could ever have seen the Lord perform.

I had been reading a book written by R. W. Schambach, a renowned preacher who for many decades walked in the Spirit. Signs and wonders frequently followed his ministry. He related a story about a young girl in his congregation in New Jersey who had been healed after a nail had been lodged in her eye. The doctors were going to remove her eye, but the Lord miraculously healed her in an instant. The story is very touching, and a must read for anyone seeking to know how God shows his love through Jesus.

It is obvious from Schambach's story, and the one I will share below, that Jesus is the same yesterday, today, and forever. Jesus is still in the healing business!

Not long ago the pastor and elders of our church commissioned the founding of a prayer team. The prayer team had been meeting in each other's homes for several years, breaking bread together, praying, and sharing God's Word.

The Holy Spirit was bonding the team, and the team's expectation that God was about to do something big kept getting stronger.

About six months ago, a two-year-old girl, Alexa, had been stabbed in the eye with a steak knife. The incident happened completely by accident. Apparently, the mother and daughter were seated next to each other at a counter. The mother had dropped her steak knife. After she picked it up from the floor, the daughter happened to lean over to see what her mother was doing. When the mother arose, the knife went right into her daughter's eye.

They rushed the daughter off to the emergency ward to see a doctor. They examined the eye and told the mother and father that there was nothing they could do. They patched the eye and sent them home with the instructions to put anti-biotics in the eye daily and return the next week for an operation to remove the eye. They said they could fix their daughter up with a glass eye.

The parents were distraught.

Fortunately, the girl's uncle was attending our church. He told the mother and father about the prayer team and encouraged them to bring Alexa to the

Saturday night service. When they arrived at church, the prayer team received word that a little girl had been stabbed in the eye and the parents were requesting prayer. When that was told to me, my spirit leaped inside. I just knew that God was going to heal this young girl! After all, I thought, God was not a respecter of persons. Would He withhold His healing power for Alexa having already healed the other little girl Schambach had prayed for? Absolutely not!

After the service, the family and relatives of this young girl were brought to the back hallway of the church. There was pandemonium in that hallway as we gathered to pray for her. People were running in all directions as they left the service, so we huddled together as they passed us by. Our church had grown so much, and the prayer team was a new entity. There was no place for us to go. But on that evening that didn't stop our faith or God.

As we gathered, I tried to encourage everyone's faith to receive by sharing the story that Schambach had told. Then the team prayed with all their hearts to the Lord on behalf of this young girl. God answered in a miraculous way. The prayer team found out later what God had done.

I heard the following story from the uncle. He said that evening after the service the mother went to put the antibiotics into her daughter's eye.

As she lifted the patch she had an idea. She thought she might hold up a ball and ask her daughter if she saw anything. She covered her daughter's other eye and held up the ball and asked her what she saw. The daughter responded, "I see a ball." The doctors said it was a miracle. They said she would have 20/20 vision, without any further problems.

Jesus said, "The works that I do you will do also." Jesus was referring to the signs and wonders He was performing. John the Baptist asked his disciples if Jesus was the Savior. Jesus told John's disciples to go and tell John that the lame walk, the blind see, and the dead are raised. Those were the works He spoke of that we as believers would do if we were true followers of Him.

About a year ago one of my employees told me that his brother was diagnosed with pancreatic cancer. He said his brother, Mike, was sent home from the hospital after the doctors told him that there wasn't anything they could do on account of the degree of advancement. He said his brother would like me to pray for him.

I called a young man who I knew was filled with the Spirit, and asked him to join me. I knew he had the faith to pray and believe for Mike's healing. The two of us went to Mike's home. My Spirit-filled friend had shared with our prayer team a vision he had one day. In it, the Lord showed him a baseball cap on a cross. The Lord revealed to him that his church was taking His Word far too casually.

When we entered Mike's house, my friend noticed a baseball cap on the table. He shared with Mike what the Lord had showed him. When he finished, we prayed for Mike. Mike was a Christian and received what my friend said and was ready for prayer. When we anointed him with oil, I recalled how Smith Wigglesworth had poured an entire bottle of oil over a sick person's head. I decided to let the oil flow and poured it all out. The person Wigglesworth had prayed for was healed, so I figured God would heal Mike too.

A couple of months passed before I got word about Mike's condition. I met his brother at work, and he told me that Mike was just fine. In fact, he had put on all the weight he had lost and was working overtime at a local warehouse.

The Bible tells us that we are to be a witness for Jesus Christ. Signs and wonders are a witness to Jesus' living presence. Kenneth Hagin said many times that healing was the dinner bell. People love miracles. People came by the thousands to see Jesus perform miracles. Paul wrote that he didn't preach the word with the wisdom of men but with demonstration and power. We are to be tabernacles of witness. Signs and wonders ought to follow the preaching of the Word today just like it did in the early church.

I hope that I have encouraged your faith. The Bible says that it is men's traditions that rob God's Word of its power. I hope you will examine yourself and see if tradition has taken a stronghold on your beliefs. Please be honest with yourself. God desires to bless you and use you. And if you do not have a relationship with the Son of God, please do something about it today. Time is short, and He is coming soon. Jesus said, "I am the way, the truth, and the life and no one comes unto the Father except through Me." He said if you don't believe Him for His Word, then believe the works He performed. He is the living God who watches over His Word and is still performing signs and wonders today.

When Jesus performed His first miracle, the changing of water to wine, He was showing us that we would become vessels filled with rivers of living water. When Jesus' mother came to Him and asked Him to do this, He told her that it was not His time. He was referring to the day He rose and sat down at the right hand of the Father. His time came when He finished His work on the cross. He was then able to be seated in heaven, where He waited for His Father to pour out the Holy Spirit. In essence, just like the bridegroom that withheld the best wine till last, our Heavenly Father withheld the outpouring of the Holy Spirit. The vessels Jesus filled with wine are examples of you and me being filled with the Holy Spirit.

There is one story I would like to share with you about how I was disobedient as a young man. My first paying job out of high school couldn't have been better. I worked for a man named Frank who owned a printing company in Minneapolis, Minnesota. Back in 1963, he hired me to take care of his yard.

He had about four acres on Christmas Lake, near the town of Excelsior. Frank not only had a big yard, he also owned several boats, and I was given the responsibility of taking care of them.

Even though he had a lot of grass to mow, there were times when he would let me ski behind his boats. He had been a huge promoter of water skiing in his youth, so he had the best of the best in skiing gear and boats. Many times, he would invite his friends over for parties. Since I had become somewhat known for my ability to barefoot ski, he would have me show off for his friends. That was a great way to cool off after mowing!

In the winter, Frank would hire a person to plow a skating rink. He would also have him shave the ice so that it was as smooth as glass. The snow and shavings were piled around the rink to form a windbreak. In the windbreak he would plant tall pine trees and string them with lights. It made a beautiful Christmas scene and beautiful rink. He would invite his friends and business associates over for ice skating parties.

One day in the middle of January, he asked me to pick up his party bus and put it out on the ice. He said he wanted to use it as a warming house for the skaters. That day, as was his custom, he gave me a list of about eleven things to do. Around eleven p.m. I arrived with the bus and put it on the lake side of the ice rink as he instructed. He also instructed me to put some two by six wood planks under the tires to spread the weight out over the ice. By now I am sure you are starting to get the picture.

It was freezing cold outside and I was exhausted from a long day's work. In order for me to get the planks, I would have had to climb the hill from the lake and go all the way to the back of his property to his remote garage.

I was nineteen years old at the time, and I thought the ice would be strong enough. After all, I had driven on the ice many times in my car and so had everyone else. So I went home that night with the fullest intention of getting up early in the morning to put the planks under the tires.

About six in the morning there was a knock on my bedroom door. It was my dad coming to tell me that I had a phone call from Frank. I asked Dad if he knew what he wanted, and Dad told me it was something about him wanting to know if I had put the planks under the tires. And then Dad said Frank wanted to know if I knew of any good wrecker companies! I about dropped to my knees. I knew just what he was talking about. I pictured his bus somewhere on the bottom of the lake.

I was afraid to pick up the phone, but finally did. Frank told me to get over to his house immediately. Fortunately, my '53 Studebaker started on that cold morning. When I arrived, Frank had already found a wrecker. They had parked the big rig on the bank and had tied its winch cable around the axle of the bus. No, the bus hadn't sunk. It was sitting on the ice, but water was up to the center of its hubcaps. It was slowly sinking. They winched it up onto more solid ice. When I saw it come out of the water, I was feeling pretty good.

Frank pointed at the bus and told me to get in it and get it off the lake. I was scared to even walk on the ice, let alone get in that bus. I ran and jumped in. Again, fortunately, the bus started. I pressed on the throttle as hard as I could and began a quarter mile trip to the pump house road. When I looked in the rearview mirror, I saw the crowd of people that had gathered to witness the resurrection of Frank's bus. They were all waving and shouting at me. I thought perhaps the lake was breaking up under the bus. When I reached the lake road I stopped the bus to find out what they were shouting about. I found the bus was on fire underneath!

I got down in the snow and looked up to see that the emergency break was burning. I couldn't believe I had forgotten to release the brake! I madly began packing snow around the drive shaft where the brake was situated. In a few minutes, the fire was out.

I had failed to obey the instructions Frank gave me. Eventually, I lost that wonderful job. Now as I look back on that incident, I can't help but think of how Moses lost the opportunity to enter the Promised Land because he too failed to obey God's instructions. God told Moses to strike the rock once, but Moses struck it twice. This angered God so much God forbade Moses from entering the Promised Land. God has promised us eternal life if we believe Jesus is His Son and that He rose from the dead. He also promises us good health and long life. The apostle John conveyed what the Holy Spirit was telling him when he told the church that God desired them to prosper and be in good health even as their souls prospered. In essence, we can live in the Promised Land right now if we are obedient.

Often God would lead me by dreams. There are two more I would like to share with you before I close. In 1986, I was looking for a building for our business. If you recall, we were in a dusty old warehouse in Avoca at the time. I had found a small steel building for sale but wasn't sure it would meet our needs. On account of the fact that it was the only one available in the area, I had prayed for guidance. In a dream that night I found myself skating along the edge of Christmas Lake. It was a lake I grew up on and was very familiar with. The best skating was in early winter when the edges were frozen. The ice would be very thin, but it didn't take much ice to hold you up. As I was skating along, I marveled at how clear the ice was because I could easily see the bottom. The bottom was less than a foot from the surface of the ice, so I wasn't too concerned about falling in. To my surprise, that is exactly what happened. I suddenly woke up.

Now this dream happened in direct response to my inquiry for guidance. It had been nearly twenty-five years since the last time I skated on that lake.

I asked God what the dream meant. My conclusion was that I would be skating on thin ice if I were to buy that building. I did not buy it, but it was just a few days later the realtor I told you about called me to tell me about the building I did buy. I believe I was listening to the voice of God and being obedient to His direction. He is no respecter of persons and will do the the same for you.

In addition to dreams to guide you, God also uses other people to encourage you and to build your faith. This story happened when my children, Erin and Brian, were about six and eight years old. We were in northern Minnesota on vacation at Dad's cabin. I had taken Brian fishing the day before and he caught a record smallmouth bass. Erin was excited about Brian's large fish, so I decided to take her fishing the next day. Brian wanted to go along too.

Brian kept saying he was going to catch an even bigger fish. We were on a lake that was part of a larger chain of lakes. This lake was unusual because the water was the color of a swimming pool, a beautiful aqua blue.

This was due to the fact that the bottom had a lot of clay in it and as a result it had very few weeds. Overhanging the lakeshore were many cedar trees, and on the banks and through the woods were many pine and birch trees.

It was a gorgeous morning. The lake was calm and the weather couldn't have been better. The boat ride took about ten minutes to reach the north end of the lake. I wanted Erin to try the same fishing hole where Brian had caught his trophy fish, which we later had mounted.

Both the kids had their lines in the water. I started the motor and began trolling about one hundred feet from the lakeshore. There was an underwater shelf where the fish liked to congregate. Brian kept saying, "I'm going to catch a bigger fish!" Shortly, he had a bite. His pole had a huge bend in it, and he began jumping up and down in the boat. I told him to settle down and wind in the fish. He said, "It's bigger than the one I had yesterday!"

Erin and I watched as he struggled with this monster. Suddenly, his line went limp. I never saw a more disappointed look on a young boy's face. He reeled in his line and found that the new artificial bait I had just bought for him was gone. This made him even more upset. I stumbled for words to help make him feel better, but then I had a moment of inspiration.

A few years earlier I had heard a story told by Charles Capps, the pastor from England, Arkansas, about a fish he had that had gotten away with his bait. He was fishing with another pastor from Little Rock, Happy Caldwell.

Both being preachers, they began to discuss the situation of the fish that had stolen his bait. Charles said something like, "Didn't God give man authority over the birds of the air and the fish of the sea?" Happy agreed that He did. So the two of them agreed that the fish would have to give the bait back to them. It wasn't but a few minutes before they heard a stirring in the water and saw that fish jump out and spit the bait back into the boat!

When I heard that story, I decided that kind of faith was way beyond my present spiritual state. I decided I would put it on a mental shelf and not think about it for a while. Now I was faced with an opportunity to teach my children about God and faith. So, in faith I told those kids Charles Capps' story. When I finished, I asked the kids if they would like to pray and believe that the fish would give us back Brian's new bait.

Both were eager to pray. Now I knew I was going out on a limb. I thought if that bait didn't show up, I would be destroying their faith in God. On the other hand, I felt sure God would answer. I prayed with the kids, and we asked God to spare that fish's life. We also asked Him to cause the fish to be able to spit out the bait and that Brian would get it back.

We sat waiting for the fish to spit the bait into the boat. We waited about ten minutes. Finally, I said let's continue fishing. So we left that spot, and I took them out into the lake further in a large sweeping circle. About fifteen minutes later we arrived back at the spot we left.

About twenty feet from the boat, I saw something floating on the water. I asked Brian to look. The object in the water had all our attention. As we approached it, I said, "Is that your bait?" Brian shouted with glee. It was his bait! We all thought it was a miracle. When we got back to the cabin, I was anxious to tell Shirley about our adventure in faith.

Sometimes when the Lord is trying to tell us something, we just don't listen.

In 1998, Shirley and I took an RV trip to Alaska. We had just purchased a new motorhome and were anxious to take it on a long trip. We signed up with Tracks to Adventure to take their Alaskan tour. We had previously taken a trip with this company to eastern Canada and had a wonderful time.

From the moment we left the house, both of us were feeling uneasy. But neither of us told the other what we were feeling. The first day out, our new motorhome was losing air in the tires. I stopped in South Dakota at an RV supply store to get a new set of tire valve extensions because the ones on the coach were bad. A couple of days later we arrived at our tour departure point, which was Canmore, British Columbia, Canada.

As we pulled into the campground, I smelled diesel fuel. I looked under the coach and saw fuel dripping from the fuel tank. I called the manufacturer of our coach and asked advice. They called me back and told me there were two tank repair companies in Canada. One was in Quebec and the other was in Calgary. Fortunately for us, Calgary was only a hundred miles east of Canmore.

We got back into the motorhome and headed to Canmore. When we were there the tank company removed the tank, welded it, and replaced it. Apparently, the manufacturer of the coach had failed to install any protective rubber between the steel straps and the aluminum tank. The straps wore holes through the aluminum. When the tank was refilled, it leaked. They had forgotten to check the other side of the tank. Two days later we were back

in Canmore, ready for our tour. The group was ready to leave the next morning.

As we left, we still had this uneasy feeling. Neither one of us thought to pray about it. When we signed up for the tour, the wagon master suggested that we should not take our tow car. He believed it would sustain damage due to the road conditions. But I had always towed a vehicle and never had any trouble. Besides, I felt we needed the Jeep in order to take side trips into the mountains and local towns. I wanted to see as much of Alaska as time warranted. So I told him we were going to pull the car.

One day we traversed many frost heaves. That was what they called the sudden rising and falling of the pavement due to frost. Later in the day, I noticed that the support tubes that attached the car hitch to the chassis of the car were broken. I caught the problem in time to have them welded. A few days later, we were descending the mountain road that led to Valdez.

It was drizzling as we descended. It was a nice two-lane highway.

In the distance coming toward us, I noticed a car flashing his lights at me. We soon passed each other, and I thought there might be an accident ahead or tree in the road. A minute or two later I looked into my rearview mirror and saw a car passing us. I thought this guy must be stupid passing us when a van was coming toward us in the opposite direction. Suddenly I heard a voice speaking to me. It said, "Look again, stupid!" I was thinking that car sure looked familiar, and when I looked it was our Jeep!

I yelled to Shirley, "Our Jeep is passing us!"

She said in disbelief, "What?"

I said, "Our Jeep is passing us!" I began flashing the lights on the motorhome at the van coming in the opposite direction and tried to stop the motorhome on the right shoulder. Time felt like an eternity as we watched that Jeep go by and watched the van coming. Fortunately, the Jeep took a veering path to the left just in time to avoid hitting the van. The Jeep went down a twelve-foot embankment and headed straight for a large cottonwood tree. I couldn't wait for the car to stop. It was a brand-new Jeep Grand Cherokee. It totaled itself against the tree doing about 55 miles an hour!

I was glad it stopped but was sickened to see such a beautiful car end up such a mess.

In the meantime, the van had swerved to miss the Jeep. It went off the side of the road and traveled through some brush. For a second it appeared on the road again and then went back into the brush. I jumped out of the motorhome and began running up the hill to see if I could find the driver of the van. I looked up and saw the man coming towards me. He was running down the hill yelling, "Are they okay?"

I said, "Who?"

He said, "The people in the car!"

I realized then that he did not know I was pulling the car. So I told him I was towing it. For a second he had a relieved look on his face and then with a frown and somewhat harsh voice said, "I hope you have good insurance!"

I thought, "Oh boy, this guy is going to sue me." His wife was also in the van but by now had arrived on the scene with her husband. Shirley and I invited them into the motorhome out of the rain. They actually turned out to be a very nice couple who lived locally.

Fortunately, they only had minor damage to their van and neither of them was hurt. The hitch had failed due to frost heaves snapping the bolts. The installer had used the wrong size bolts when the hitch was installed. The Jeep was totaled and ended up in a junkyard in Juneau.

The next day Shirley and I noticed something different. The uneasy feeling we had been having was gone. Shirley and I had been at odds with each other from the time we left the house. Little things kept bothering us and we were short with each other. Suddenly, the oppression left. We told each other how we had been feeling and it was then we realized that we had missed God's warning. When we leave home, we always ask God to bless our trip. We had done so on this trip, but we did not respond to His Spirit until after the accident. The rest of the trip was peaceful.

Jesus told us to ask Him anything, and as long as it was in agreement with His Word He would do it. He said that if we asked Him He would do it so that our joy would be full. On one occasion, on another RV trip, we had another mishap and we needed His help. We had just left an RV show in Indianapolis, Indiana. We stopped for the night in Frankenmuth, Michigan.

We had called ahead and made reservations at the Yogi Bear Campground.

Shirley asked if they had space for a forty-foot motorhome towing a car, and they said they did.

When we arrived, we were assigned a camping space. I could see I was going to have great difficulty turning into that space. There were little posts next to the road that marked the camping sites. I tried for ten minutes to make that motorhome fit but was unsuccessful.

On one attempt I was backing up and Shirley was

standing behind the motorhome waving me backwards. I was concerned about the post on the passenger side so I looked up to see if my front tires would miss. At the moment I looked up, Shirley waved for me to stop. I didn't see her. When I did, she was madder than a hornet. She was shaking her head and saying something I couldn't hear. I knew I had done something wrong.

I got out of the motorhome to take a look. Lying on the back of the coach was the left side of a guy's awning. I had caught the corner of his awning, and it slid up the back of the coach. putting a one-foot scratch in the paint. The awning, on the other hand, appeared to be in good condition. I asked Shirley to check with the campground and see if we could get assigned to another site. She did, and we moved to the new site which was negotiable.

The people who owned the camping trailer whose awning I backed into were not home at the time. So after setting up in the new campsite I decided to walk down to the trailer to see if they were back. As I approached the trailer, I heard the two of them shouting and yelling at each other. They were in a big fight over something. As I approached the site the man threw open the trailer door. In doing so the top corner of the door caught the awning canvas and ripped a two-foot-long hole.

He saw me standing there, a place I did not want to be

at the time. He said in a very gruff voice, "What do you want?" For a second I didn't know what to say but then I told him I'd had an accident with his awning. He vented a little and then said, "I don't need any more problems today!" I told him what had happened and handed him my business card. I told him that if he found anything wrong, I would be happy to pay him for his expenses.

A few days later, Shirley and I were spending some time at our cabin on Bluewater in Minnesota. The phone rang and it was this guy from Michigan. He said, "Mr. Sage, I figured out how much you owe me. It will be $600.00."

I was speechless but when I found my voice I said, "Okay, I will send you

a check." I hung up the phone and found Shirley. I told her what the man had said. I asked her if she would join me in prayer. I felt this man was trying to get into our pocketbook. We both prayed and asked the Lord to rectify the situation.

The next day, the man called me back. His story was amazing. He said, "Mr. Sage, I have been thinking about what I said yesterday. I hadn't fully set up the awning, so the damage caused when I opened the door wasn't your fault. I checked the brackets, and I thought one was bent but I can buy one for about $5.00 at the local RV store. But would you please send me $50.00 so I can make it up to my wife by taking her out to dinner?" I told him I would send him the $50.00 and I did. I hope he and his wife were happy, because Shirley and I were filled with joy!

Talk about being filled with joy, I wish you could have been with us on our first Christmas celebration in our new home on Beaver Lake. Shirley and I were having fun taking videos of Brian and Erin as they opened their presents. Brian was three and half years old and Erin was one and a half.

Have you ever had a time in your life when your spirit just leaps within you?

That was the moment we caught on tape as Brian opened his most prized present. We had bought him a toy workbench. When he opened the present and saw the workbench, he yelled out in the cutest sweetest voice: "SKWOOS AND SKWOODRIVERS!" He was absolutely enthralled with that present. Nothing compared to the joy he experienced when he opened that one gift.

I remember thinking, that boy is going to be mechanically inclined just like his father, grandfather, and great grandfather. I recalled that I also had such a moment like that the first time my dad took me to see my grandfather's factory. My grandfather, L.F. Norris, was an inventor and manufactured milk dispensers in Minneapolis, Minnesota.

I can still recall that wonderful day when I was only eight years old and Dad took me into that building. As we walked through the office area, Dad opened a door that led out into the manufacturing section. The first thing I saw were large stainless-steel boxes rolling down a conveyor line. Upon seeing them, my spirit jumped on the inside of me. I was thrilled with what my eyes were beholding.

We walked down the line and around the end. Then Dad took me into the parts room. Again, my spirit rose up inside of me. I enjoyed looking at all the parts on the shelves. I didn't know at the time that someday I would be manufacturing products later in life, but I certainly have never forgotten that day.

Then I was young and now I am older. I realize now that on that day God was speaking to me. It was as if He was saying, "Son, someday you will be making machines that make life better." In fact, the slogan on our brochures says, "Products that make life better." Today, of course, I regret the foolish things I did in my youth. But the Bible cautions us not to look back but to press forward. It teaches us that once we have been born again old things have passed away and all things have become new. We are new creatures in Christ and are made the righteousness of Christ in God.

If you recall, my dad passed away in March of 1982, just two months after my grandmother died. For several years, I was concerned about whether or not my dad had been born again. The Bible is quite clear that a person must be born again in order to enter the Kingdom of Heaven.

God knew that my heart was troubled over this concern. One night in 1987, I had a dream about my earthly father. In that dream, I found myself standing in a corridor. It was one that led to a large stadium, like a football stadium. Looking towards the field, all I could see was an extremely bright light. I could not see the bleachers on the other side on account of the light being too bright. I sensed in my spirit that Jesus was standing in the middle of that field and that He was the reason for the brightness of the light.

I was standing close to the opening of the corridor that led to the bleachers very high up in the stadium. Next to me were about a dozen men and women putting on white gowns. I turned and looked down the corridor because I heard a familiar voice. It was dark at that end, so I couldn't make out who was coming towards me. As he approached, I said, "Dad, is that you?" He kept coming closer, and as he did he was quoting a passage of scripture. I replied again with, "Dad, is that you?" He repeated the scripture, and this time I could make out his image. It was my dad. My spirit was leaping inside me with joy. As I looked at him, I noticed that he wasn't the overweight sixty-three-year-old man as I had last seen him. Instead, he was tall and thin like he was when I was eight years old.

I said in frustration, "I can't remember what you are telling me." I turned to the man next to me and asked him if he could understand what my dad was telling me. He shook his head and continued dressing. Then Dad and I were standing face to face. I said one more time, "I can't remember what you are telling me."

He looked at me and said in a very loving voice, "Just remember Wings of Fire." After he said that, he turned around and disappeared. This dream happened long before Promise Keepers began meeting in football stadiums. You can imagine the joy I felt when I first heard about them.

In the morning, I recalled every detail of that dream. It was finally settled in my heart that Dad was born again. To hear him quoting scripture was verycomforting to my soul. I began a search of the Bible to see if I could find out what Dad was quoting. He used the expression "Wings of Fire" to refer to the passage he was quoting. I believe the passage referred to a coming event. I could not find those words tied together in any passage. As of today, I am still waiting on the Lord to reveal what this means.

The prophet Isaiah said, "They that wait upon the Lord

shall mount up on WINGS as eagles.".", And the apostle John wrote, "He that comes after me will fill you with the Holy Spirit and FIRE," I believe the Holy Spirit is saying to the church, "Prepare to mount up on WINGS OF FIRE." I believe He is commanding us to walk in the anointing He has poured out upon us. Acts 1:8 KJV says, "But ye shall receive power, after that the Holy Ghost is come upon you..."

One of my favorite scripture's is Hebrews 11:6 KJV. "But without faith it is impossible to please him: for he that cometh to God must believe that he is, and that he is a rewarder of them that diligently seek him."

Timing is everything. Jesus knew the times. He knew when it was His time to lay down His life and when to pick it up again. He knew when to change the water to wine and when to pour out His Holy Spirit. Now is the time for the body of Christ to be fitly joined together to rise up in the anointing God has given it. It is time to put on the anointing and mount up on Wings of Fire!

God has a time for everything. I am sure you have heard many times the expression "He was in the right place at the right time." I was certainly in the right place at the right time when I started the Mart Cart business. I was able to pioneer this field of caregiving. Although we were tested many times, we did not fall. On one occasion during our first expansion of the Mart Cart building, I had two dealers steal from me. They had purchased about 40 carts from us. They sold them to local grocery stores and never paid us.

I needed the money to pay the construction company for the expansion work. Unable to collect, I went to the guys doing the work and told them the story. They agreed to work with me for 90 days. God supplied all I needed in that period of time.

Another product line we developed was Jotto Desk. It was another matter of being at the right place at the right time. One day I was sitting in the local coffee shop, Marion's Donuts, in Rogers. I had been there many times over the years. I had been asking the Lord to use me to share the gospel with someone. In my heart I wanted to help someone by sharing what the Lord had done for me.

As I was sipping a cup of coffee, I noticed a deputy sheriff seated at a table near by. I felt the urge to get up and go sit across from him. I introduced myself and he told me his name. We hit it off right and over the course of time he began to share what was going on in his life. He began to tell me that his wife had run away with another man and that he was in terrible financial condition. I knew God had an answer for him, and I was eager to share what He had done for me.

A few months later, after our relationship had grown, he came into Marion's and asked me to come and see what he had made for his police car. I went outside to take a look and saw a very nice desk he had made. He used some two inch exhaust pipe to support a plexiglass desk top. On top

he had mounted several spring-loaded clips to hold various items. It was well organized. He told me he had been in a car chase one day and while negotiating a corner at high speed everything on the seat of the car flew onto the floor. He decided to make a desk to support everything. He also said that he had sold some to his fellow officers.

This deputy had seen a need and filled it. I, on the other hand, was anxious to help him get out of his financial woes. I wanted to bless him, so I told him he had made a wonderful product and asked him if he would allow me to work on his design to improve it. I wanted to make the desk more ergonomic and more versatile. He trusted me and gave me his consent.

I went back to my engineering room at Assembled Products Corporation and spent the next year trying to enhance the deputy's design. I worked with many of our suppliers and relied on their input. After a year's time went by, I felt sure we had a product that could be sold in large quantities. All the while, its inventor was watching intently, and was very excited about what was happening.

We named the new desk "Jotto Desk" coming from "jot and auto." The design was so unique we hired a patent attorney and in time received a patent. We had a new stand that would telescope and a new desktop that was made from molded plastic. It would swivel at the top to make it more ergonomic.

The deputy-turned-inventor was anxious to come and work for us. I told him we would hire him once the product took hold and we were generating an income. In the meantime, I offered to pay him a royalty on every desk we sold. He was excited about his future. For the first time, I could see hope in his eyes and hear it in his voice.

We took the desk to the SEMA convention in Las Vegas. The desk was a new item to that industry and once again we were pioneering a new concept.

Sales started slowly, but over the next couple years they began to grow. The deputy was getting more and more excited until one day he just quit his job with the sheriff's department and showed up at the door. It was time to hire.

You could never have asked for a better person to represent the Jotto Desk.

He was perfect for all customer service inquires and support.

In those days, personal computers were just beginning

to come to market. Our sales team was getting requests for something to hold them in the car.

The person whom we had given responsibility of marketing and sales over Jotto Desk came to me one day to tell me what we needed.

He had a gift of being able to sort and assimilate knowledge.

He was also a Spirit-filled believer and was confident that we could sell many more desks if we designed something that could hold computers.

In my mind, I could see dozens of computers of all different sizes and thicknesses. To me, clamps would not be very feasible. So I felt we needed to use some other method to hold them down. I suggested I believed that if we used thin vinyl coated aircraft cables, we could fit any size computer we needed to, and we would be able to keep the weight of the desk to a minimum.

Our salesman thought that would work, and so I began designing a new desktop. It wasn't long before we had a new plastic molded desk that was able to do just what we wanted it to do. And it wasn't long after that that we had another patent.

The timing for Jotto Desk was perfect. We were in the market at the right time and at the right place. Today, thousands of desks leave our facility every month. The deputy is blessed beyond his imagination. He says that coming to work is like going on vacation.

God has certainly answered my questions about life and my reason for being. He has filled me with inexpressible joy. I no longer search for my reason for being or why the universe was created. I know it was all for God's glory and out of His love was it made. It is for us to enjoy. But we have an enemy, the devil, who would destroy us if he could. But he has been defeated. We have God on our side, and if God be for us then who can be against us?

Permissions:

Mart Cart™, Spray Master Technologies™, Jotto Desk-™, and Assembled Products™ Corporation used by permission of Assembled Products™ Corporation, Rogers, Arkansas.

Bibliographical references:

Hagin, Kenneth. *I Believe in Visions.* Old Tappan, 1972.

Printed in the USA
CPSIA information can be obtained
at www.ICGtesting.com
CBHW051953121124
17306CB00002B/3